Management Book - International Best Seller

The Lion & the Guru

The amazing story of becoming a team leader

Daniel Andrino

Dedicated to my family

Testimonials

"In the book I found a perspective of leadership that breaks the vision of the leader born or made, giving prominence to the personnel decision. That leadership has multiple styles, which is best suited for each situation and very visual examples in order to remember the message that make this book a practical and recommended reading. "

Senior Manager Cap Gemini

"Those people, whose career path has led them to the enormous and fascinating responsibility of leadership, know that to get people to develop and draw from them more than what they themselves have even thought they could give, you have to be constantly performing and making an effort to adapt to the characteristics of each of them. There is more than one style of leadership, and those who consider it as such and act on it, will never be recognized as leaders. This adaptability requires great skills, the more you train the more you discover what is needed. The author, through this ingenious fable refreshes us and forces us to review and consider whether we are acting correctly in each situation, and with a valuable pragmatic approach, offers it to us, veterans and newcomers in the art of directing an epilogue where he concludes and summarizes to offer us a tool to use regularly."

Finance Director - Securitas Direct

"During the reading of *The Lion and the Guru*, at different times, you see a reflection of your work and personal life. No doubt after reading it, success in life or lack thereof is in everyone's hand."

Area Manager - Walt Disney Studio Motion Pictures

"It is a useful work for executives and consultants and all professionals interested in developing their leadership skills. Daniel discusses the cornerstones of leadership, in a pleasant and easy to understand manner. He gives practical examples that make viewing basic concepts, which because they are simple, are not less important."

"In my experience I have found that those who have the skill to simplify things achieve effective results and are carriers of success."

HR Portugal & Greece - Cisco

"This book provides the reader a fun way to learn, from animal behavior, leadership skills, structured on a conceptual model that is easy to apply. Learn to lead any kind of animal you find in your office."

HR Manager - Uralita

"This original work invites us to travel across the world of people discovering that volume units are physical quantities that we have to overcome since the dimensions of the individual are unlimited and there is always room for improvement, learning and getting ahead." Once again the West has to learn from African wisdom, which is based on the living encyclopedias; these are the wisest."

Academic Coordinator - IDDI

"I recognize many of the criteria of leadership learned in my career, but very exemplary and concentrated in the final summary."

Corporate Resources General Director – Isolux Corsan

"How amusing way to reflect on leadership issues!"

Director – IESE Business School

Prologue

I first read this story in a Frankfurt-Madrid flight when it was still a set of loose sheets. My intention was to take an initial look and finish it later at home in my spare time or during the weekend. I couldn't. I was hooked. I devoured it during flight without blinking an eye. When I was landing in Barajas, I admit that I looked out the window to enjoy its conclusions.

The author, Daniel Andrino, gives us with this book, a great adventure story and a new management model with eight styles and forty characteristics of leadership, all extracted from the womb of nature, based on observation, the experience and expertise of his characters.

The author has had the cunning to hear the call of nature and to put on paper its universal message of leadership and team management. In addition, the model proposed here is already a novelty in itself, both for its eight styles, compared to four from Blanchard or six from Goleman, as well as the original way of creating and transmitting them, as if it were a coaching session, which is quite innovative.

Therefore, this debut characteristic adds a breath of fresh air to the existing literature on the subject of management, with a sober, simple, direct and provocative style, telling a funny story and natural, entailing a great deal of learning. Out of all the characters, Jumbe stands out as a major player, and a total catalyst of the basic pillars of co-existence and functioning of the natural order which are applicable to both the business world and to the very society in which we live. Every character, every situation and every scene has its own meaning and translation into the real world. In particular, I'll stick with Mwalimu figure, a real coach. He is the one that helps tourists discover cultural booty rough trip. How Mwalimu pinpoints this story of leadership is a real treat, even when it is a story of life and nature at heart. Best of all is that the reader will leave read and thought.

Enrique Serrano Montes

Telco, Media & Technology Director - Telvent

Jumbe

"It's all planned." said Elizabeth; the travel agent who works with our multinational company. "You'll have no problem there".

I remembered her words just at the same moment I remembered those of Kenneth, the consultant that advised me months before taking the trip: "The real leader faces uncertainty. If there is no insecurity, there is no leadership, as there is no day without night. What really matters is not to be perfect, but to know that you are imperfect and what's missing."

Then, I could not agree more with him: "True," I replied. We get trained for years, decades, and we think we know, but it is useless knowledge." I myself have studied two careers and obtained two masters. I've even lost track of the courses, seminars and conferences I have attended, and I still feel incomplete. I lack some skills or as consultants put it, skills that I think I need.

Then it was clear because if there was a place where I could feel insecure and was aware of my shortcomings, it was there and then. Of course, if that was the idea, I had succeeded.

I was seven thousand miles from my office and twenty from a phone (I am the one who never leaves my two phones, rain or shine), sitting in the front right seat of an old jeep where all those stains went unnoticed among many others. It was one of those SUV's that you're sure will not break down precisely because of its sturdiness. The driver, Mbuto Misaro, was a youth of the area, a clear example that life does deal the same cards to all. Physically, he was a prodigy, and I am sure that his intelligence far exceeded that of our pampered kids who go to expensive distinguished schools.

As it was agreed in the package tour, we were out at dawn to the game reserve where elephants could be photographed with my newly purchased digital camera, equipped with a 15x telephoto lens and enough megapixels to make a mural print.

Several decades ago, wealthy managers of the "civilized" world came to this place to hunt them and extract their teeth, and then hung them as trophies in their homes and offices. Today, savage poaching has made it necessary to ban this practice. However, for me, the interesting thing was not to acquire a trophy, but to see them in their own habitat.

"Animals do not study. They learn." Said another consultant; somebody named Robert. That was the straw that broke the camel's back and made me leave. I knew that regardless of how many books I read, how many courses I took, this could

10

only improve my life. So I said:"Why not?" I had accumulated six years without a vacation and could afford the trip. Either way, though I would not learn anything, I could use some getting-away, and of course, that goal seemed attainable in that place.

From the rustic window of the jeep, which would lower manually if it were not blocked by all the dust accumulated while racking through those roads, there was spectacular scenery in sight. A large meadow dotted by clusters of trees stretching to the horizon, where a ridge stood blurred by the huge distance. Only the road that was blazed by the continuous passage showed the existence of human beings. Miles of undisturbed nature, no man, no houses, no factories, no buildings, nothing. How wonderful!

Seventy or eighty minutes went by which I noticed in that Rolex that I received as a reward for achieving a 22 percent result over last year's objectives. A watch that I loved and feared because I saw my success in it; but it also reminded me of the 206 layoffs that had to perform when the factory was relocated.

The road was beautiful, ethereal, like another life. I had fallen deep in the light of nature until Mbuto muttered a simple "we have arrived" and I awoke from the trance. I was bewitched by that unknown Africa. I always thought that documentaries were fine until I got there. Nothing could convey the sense that Africa produces.

Mbuto pointed his strong arm to a place in the vastness and nodded as if he knew where we were going. We left the road and navigated between the bumps of the ground swaying in the jeep. It looked more like a carnival ride than a transport vehicle, but it was fun. At that time not thinking about risk, I just got carried away.

Gradually we moved into the plains to reach a set of dense trees and bushes. We slowed down until we were halfway motionless. We stood a moment in silence, waiting, as if we wanted to reassure all the life we had disturbed in its world. I was mesmerized watching every tree, every bush. The guide turned his huge ivory smile at me, and that hit me like a starting gun. It was time. Mentally I reviewed my team, I had everything I needed, and in fact I would swear that I brought a lot of extra things. That store clerk made a killing with me, advising me, as if he were an expert, about "all the possible junk that only an expert could offer, who had never gone on an adventure journey."

I opened the door slowly and pointed my adventure boots, on the adventure socks that were shown under the removable multi-pocket pants, breathable fabric, in which I carried a utility knife, a reflector, a compass and water purification tablets, carrying, in addition, the light water flask at the waist, a matching shirt, with an ammunition carrier, and vest that was seemed to be for fishing rather than for photography. The Indiana Jones of management had reached the prairie.

I followed Mbuto into the trees, away from the jeep, which seemed to be abandoned in that area. We walked a few hundred yards under the sun until reaching the first trees. Behind them, as a natural border, we found a more humid area. A small accumulation of water had attracted several elephants, frolicking in the mud. Some birds were perched on them and pecked at their skin, which the elephants seemed to ignore. It was beautiful. The image conveyed the comfort of a family portrait. I connected my digital camera and shot several times feeling a little guilty, as if stole an intimate moment. I counted six individuals, five adults and a young one. One of them remained out of the water, watching the others and, simultaneously, the surroundings. From time to time it made some noise or gesture and the rest seemed to elude him. I was attracted to his position, far and near to the rest. Absent and present, he seemed to know everything and all of them gave him their trust. That must be the leader.

We adopted a defensive posture, crouched behind the bush and approached the herd as much as possible. Just fifteen steps between us. From there, his image was more extraordinary. About the size of a truck or small bus with his legs resembling logs and their trunks looked like a husky tool. I felt my heart beating while Mbuto silenced me with a worldwide known gesture. It had been a long time since I felt that tingle. The feeling of helplessness that animal forced me to stay tuned to my movements. This was a feeling that I had lost with the arrogance of my job.

Suddenly, something happened. The great elephant tensed his muscles and issued a warning sound; the others acted immediately and began marching towards us. My eyes, watching the scene through the LCD screen of the digital camera, took a second to understand it was real. When I looked over it, four elephants were glued to us. The first two went side by side, so I stood in the middle of their path. I felt like I was between two railroad tracks, and two merchandise convoys were passing by. Mbuto had tried to catch up to me in order to protect me, but his action ran into the trunk of a third elephant, which turned him up in the air and threw him back four yards away from his path. I was paralyzed, unable to believe what was happening, and I felt the ground vibrate under my feet when the young elephant hit me. I felt a pop in my right leg, and I felt it had turned more than the body allows it. At that time, my body lost balance and lacking support, fell. On the floor, I could see my companion lying, unconscious, while the leader of the pack went between us slightly pushing the other animal, walking slower due to all the mud that had adhered to its thighs. From underneath its image was even more colossal.

And just then, a great fear came upon me: What had made them flee? A roaring and powerful sound answered my question. I would have thought that this was not real if not for the knee pain. I turned my head slowly to the small lake in fear of discovering what I already knew. On the other side, three lionesses approached with an arrogant air. They roared, and jumped, making small runs; they made sure they were noticed. Never did they look dangerous when I saw them in the 42 inches of my television in my room, but here, this was a very different thing. Their roar overwhelmed my body and looking at their mouths crippled my mind. I remembered at that time images of lions hunting antelope, lions hunting zebras, and blood, a lot, too.

Then it happened. I heard a rustling behind me and turned my head instinctively. In front of me, at about five yards, a great lion stared at Mbuto, who stood motionless on the floor. It moved closer and sniffed around. I smelt the flesh and blood that flowed through his head. I do not know what I thought. Rather, I believe that I was not thinking at all. I shouted instinctively as loud as I could, and I threw my camera towards the animal, as I stood on my left leg. I turned to yell even louder. The lion answered with a roar that shook me. I opened my arms and cried desperately. This was a daring, suicidal action, a headlong rush. I really wanted to finish me off quickly, but the lion seemed to relax. It muttered a few times and looked me up and down as if weighing if I posed a danger, though, clearly, I was not. It walked towards me and passed me in the direction towards the lionesses that waited in the lagoon. I collapsed to the floor, trembling, exhausted, but before I lost consciousness I saw that Mbuto was looking at me.

White. That's my first memory when I opened my eyes. A white roof after a soft white cloth acting as a mosquito net on a metal bed painted white. White sheets on my leg covered in plaster, also white. No doubt it was a hospital.

There was Mbuto, watching me with the teeth of his big smile. I saw in his face that he was sincerely glad for my awakening.

"Hello!" He said, and I replied with an eye blink. "You are in the Saint George Hospital in Morogoro. I brought you in yesterday, after the accident, and you were sedated due to the pain in your leg. I have also notified the agency."

Instinctively, I looked at my leg, and he returned my action:

"Do not worry. You injured your knee. The Doctor said that you will be walking in a week. Now, you need rest."

"Thanks," I replied.

"No, I thank you. You saved me."

The truth is that I had not thought that I had saved him, the same way I did not think at that time that I had.

"While you are here, I must help you. Do you want anything?"

"No, I do not know. Only chatting, I guess. What can I do?"

"Precisely, my father wants to talk to you. He is out of room because he wants to know you. My father came from the mountains when he knew about this."

"Horror!" I thought. I imagined a family crowd entertaining me, smiling with a stupid look.

"Ugh, I don't know if I should... Tell him you need not thank me for anything; I did what I had to do."

"He knows. He is not coming to thank, but to know. He is very special. He is an important person in our country. Twenty years ago, when I was child, he met Jumbe. Jumbe is the lion that attacked us. The leader of the menagerie. Many years ago that lion approached him. Looked at him. They looked at each other and..."

"And?"

"Well, he says that he spoke to him. Both are almost friends. He is a legend of our country. Since then, the tribes hear the advice of my father. Nothing is done without his input. Here we know him as Mwalimu, let's say, this is what you call an advisor. Now he wants to talk to you. I truly believe that he will not go away until you do. I know him well and he is very patient."

Wow! So the *consultants* were chasing me even to Africa. In short, I had nothing to do and nothing to lose, so... I agreed to meet the Mwalimu. "He will be like an executive coach." I thought.

Mbuto left the room and after a few minutes, entered holding the door to let his father in. He was a tall man, walking slowly, emphatically; one of those who make people shut up when he enters a room. His complexion was even darker than Mbuto's, but not enough to hide a few wrinkles that were drawn around his large and prominent lips. He had a strong, direct look, and was directed immediately to my eyes.

"Congratulations, Jumbe has chosen you. He illuminated you."

I was surprised, because his English was much better than his son's. It was definitely a talented family, though he did not dress as a westerner, but wore a kind of red robe and a large wooden necklace that hung over his chest. Certainly, he looked older than he did.

"The lion is a role model and a guide. The light." He observed again, trying to get answers.

"It is a great and beautiful animal." Was all I could muster as an answer.

18

"It's much more than that. Look at your own culture. In your culture, there is a horoscope, Leo, which considers with the brightest time of the year for you. Even the name comes from the ancient term, Lux."

"Well, if you say so;" I tried to patronize, so as not to discuss; "but I do not know what the lion wanted from me."

"Then we'll have to find out. For some reason, he has seen you and left you. He has agreed that you are a worthy rival. What do you do?"

"I run a company.

"And brings you to Africa?"

"The truth is I do not know. I came to try to discover myself. To think what I have to do for people to follow me."

"I understand, then you are like the lion. The lion rules the jungle. The savanna without the lion would be chaos. We can learn a lot from him and from nature. I imagine that your company is large."

"Yes, a lot, and growing. It has reached such a size that is very difficult to control. I understand numbers, including processes, but people are hard to convince."

"People are like water, always taking the easy path. But it is not easy to achieve. Many years ago, they came to solve the drought. They brought machines and many men who clogged the river. They wanted to contain him, but he, like people, found another way and disappeared. Now we have to make big holes. To govern a river you cannot plug it and much less go against it. We must study the current and make small changes with the appropriate materials."

"Certainly, now I have a great river that does not go where I want and I don't know what to do. I think I'm incapable of doing it."

"The lion does not think so. He has seen something in you. I can tell how he governs the jungle if it helps."

"Well, I think it might be interesting and also I have nothing to do."

"Gentlemen, I think it's time to let the patient rest." Said the British-looking doctor who had just walked into the room.

"I will return tomorrow." The tribe consultant said politely, bidding goodbye.

II.

The seven nyoka

That sunrise in Africa was far from the glamour seen in the movies, it was pure imagination. I assumed that the sun would rise slowly in the endless blue sky of the majestic horizon of the savannah. I imagined acres of pristine land that, little by little, were illuminated by the clear light rays of the sun. I imagined the purity of a landscape not yet invaded by industry. However, there I was, lying on a hospital bed; I could not be in a much uglier place and that was making my condition even crueler. I always thought that disease was an attack on human dignity. In my mind, man was born to build something. We all had a purpose to serve, and disease was nothing but an obstacle in that path. I remembered when I was young and thought that sleep and even eating were a waste of time. How wrong I was! The subsequent years showed me that resting and recharging were essential for efficiency.

After having tasteless coffee and juice for breakfast, with a couple of cookies hygienically packed, I thought back on how cold it were the hospitals. They make you understand exactly what it means to be an object. When you are in a hospital you are only products of their treatments and operations. They treat us, examine us and, ultimately, manipulate us as objects. It is rare to find someone who realizes that what is in there, bedridden, is a person. When that happens, it is usually a rookie. I guess time makes them insensitive, and they only see their activity as "part of the job."

The same feeling I have seen in many teams, the feeling that I have always hated so much. I remember a phrase the Human Resources Director, Lydia, told me when I started my job: "Do not look for work you enjoy, but enjoy the work you do." That phrase has haunted me forever, since I found it and still find it to be very wise. Everyone can find positive aspects in work and find areas to improve. Otherwise, one will just have a reactive attitude. No one knows our job better than ourselves.

Shortly after the nurse removed my breakfast tray, Mwalimu appeared. Really I welcomed the visit because that morning did not offer me a very entertaining picture. After asking about my condition, he sat down and started talking.

"They say it's best to start at the beginning, so I will tell the story in which Jumbe, the lion leader, began his leadership. Jumbe was a handsome specimen who was born in the rainy season. Gradually, he went to acquire his muscles in fights with other cubs in the pack. Then, when he was 10 years old, he became a powerful animal that was increasingly more independent. The lionesses, that once despised and mistreated him, showed interest and tried to present him with the food they caught in their hunts. This did not go unnoticed by the rest, so that the male of the pride, Kun began to watch him suspiciously. When he discovered that a member of the pride was approaching Jumbe he would approach quickly and push him away with threats or by force. Jumbe soon found himself alone in the group. No one played with him, no one competed. He had to eat leftovers from the others or hunt his own food. However, he endured long months watching. His image lurking in the bushes watching the evolution of the pride, the attacks on other species, the search for water, the violent games of the smaller lions, and above all, his constant observation of other animals and their behavior, became a daily routine in the jungle.

Then I was a young man, as now my son is, and worked as msaada or assistant at the resort. There, I learned English. One day two members of my tribe told me the story of the lone lion because, they said, he was like me, who had left the tribe. So I became interested in him. I went to see him so many times that I think he got used to see me, in the distance.

Soon, Kun decided to take action on the matter, and his rejection was more direct. It was evident that he feared that Jumbe would soon attain sufficient strength to seize the position. He knew that as Jumbe was growing, he was becoming increasingly weak. He had kept his harem for many seasons, but the day was not far off when the females would prefer a more aggressive male. So one morning I was watching the pride from a distance, he rose slowly, as he used to, and walked laying his huge paws on the dry soil of the savanna. The sun was shining brightly making waves in the horizon. The pride was under the shadow of the stylized acacias. Jumbe did not move, lying down, waiting for the boss to approach. He could have fled or could have confronted him. But he waited. Kun was not sure how to react, so he approached with caution fearing any movement. He seemed more scared than Jumbe. When he was a few inches near, his body tensed and let out a roar that stopped all the creatures in the area, including me. For a moment, there was silence. He arched his back and folded his joints just enough to be quite tense, as if cocking a gun. Jumbe did not stop staring at him and raised his face with scorn. He was neither afraid, nor wanting to attack. Kun lunged at him striking him in the head. Both rolled in the attack. I could hardly tell which was which, they were clawing each other and the blows were so strong that they sounded like two cars colliding. A cloud of dry dust hung in the air until there was silence. I was about 200 yards from them, surprised and nervous about what I had just watched. Then I saw Jumbe's back, looking sadly at the rest. Kun watched him trying to stay upright; he breathed deeply, with difficulty. My impression is that Jumbe was cooler and could resume the fight or even win it without difficulty. However, he knew he could not. He was not ready to lead the pride. That had been a mere show to justify his departure. He could neither have abandoned them, nor win. The pride needed a leader, and he could have no doubts or nominations for that purpose. He knew it was not yet time.

He walked for several days wandering with the only company of a young man, at a distance, watching him as a mere pastime. The truth is that I did not have much to do and that seemed fun. His fate led him to the Mlima foothills, the mountains of the southern savanna. A strange place, as few animals go there. Mlima is a rocky place where many birds come to lay their eggs in the breeding season. I think Jumbe went there precisely because he knew that the pride would never go there. Perhaps he was drawn to see something different.

Mlima, at the time, was an inhospitable place, but when we arrived, we could see that it was worse than I expected. Along the access road, dozens of animals laid dead. Bodies of birds, mammals, herbivores, spread over the rocks or sand. Some seemed to have been there for some time. Others were recent. That was the scene of an indiscriminate massacre. Then I started to worry because I knew that there were few animals living in the area, and I was not a difficult prey. Jumbe had looked at me a couple of times during the journey, but more to let me know that he knew I was there than to attack me, however now in a place where food was scarce, he might well consider that possibility.

He spent the night there, and I got an old mte, a tree from which he could see the rock formation. A young lion as Jumbe could easily climb the tree, but at least, it would be a little hard for him. At night the place was mysterious. The rocks seemed to absorb some of the moon's light and the semi-darkness lingered about the place allowing distinguishing shadows. The silence was overwhelming. Just before dawn, I was awakened by a roar. Jumbe was being attacked.

From that tree, I could not see anything, but listened to the lion moving with agility among the rocks. At first, I thought he had become crazy or had a nightmare, a sleep-walking lion.

I could not wait any longer; I was so curious that I inadvertently climbed down the tree to get close to the area. The sun had appeared on the horizon, and its rays began to illuminate the rocks. Jumbe jumped from one to another looking at the floor. When I was a few yards from him, he raised his face and looked at me. Then I realized that I was wrong. Being carried away by curiosity, I had gotten close enough to invade his comfort zone. In two jumps, he stood before me, jumping over a rock, which was about a yard tall, ready to attack. I closed my eyes, but I held my ground and stood straight up. I stood in fear. I really thought that was the end.

Jumbe stood there, a few centimeters from me. I looked at him. He was looking down. Under his paw a nyoka, there was a rock python, trying to get free. My legs were shaking, but it seemed that Jumbe did not see me. It was as if for him, I did not exist and yet, he just saved my life, for that nyoka could have poisoned me with a single bite. He turned his mane slowly and glared at me. It was but a moment, and enough to make acknowledge it.

I stepped back and Jumbe raised his paw. The rock python, freed from the weight, zigzagged quickly to get away from the lion. When it was two yards away, it turned and tried to stand, but Jumbe jumped towards it. The snake ducked its head, hit the floor and fell into a hole in the rock, while nervously, sticking his forked tongue in and out. As soon as it entered the hole, Jumbe moved a rock with his paw to cover it and prevent it from coming back out.

Then he walked quietly to another path between the rocks. I peered around from the height without moving a muscle.

A quick move caught my attention again. Again, he was facing a snake. It was a sight unknown. I never thought this could happen, but it did. Jumbe was dancing face to face with another python. The tapered face of the serpent stood proudly before the cat and agile launched attacks against him. The lion was totally focused on the movements of the reptile masterfully dodging them. With small jumps, he surrounded the snake, which followed his path with sudden attack movements. It launched its jaws with sharp teeth against the face of the cat. He jumped to one side, and the snake immediately coiled to get back on guard. This was repeated several times lasting milliseconds. When Jumbe learned the rhythm of the movement, he went on the attack and with an accurate bite, caught the serpent's head in his mouth. He raised his head and the rest of the python was moving in the air as it were the lion's tong. However, there he had no intention of biting or swallowing, just stayed with the rock python in his mouth until the snake was completely motionless. A few seconds later, he opened his jaw and dropped the frightened snake, which sat motionless on the rock. Jumbe pushed it with his front leg to a crack between two huge rocks and blocked the exit with another stone.

Jumbe spent several hours locating the rest of the snakes in the area and fighting with them. Each snake was enclosed in different holes in the rock. Without doubt, the landscape littered with corpses was a result of their voracity. For a long time, the snakes had been hunting indiscriminately for no apparent reason.

It was clear they had not killed those animals to satisfy their hunger, but only because they had crossed their path. Now he had removed that threat."

"What happened to them?" I asked with genuine interest.

"Well, the story does not end here. I spent the night on that rock. It was a place that did not really protect me from the lion or the snakes. However, I felt safe. I sensed that Jumbe would attack me and even prevent another animal from doing so.

In the morning the lion ate the remains of one the nearby victims and then headed to the crack where it had the first snake was trapped. With little effort he freed it from its confinement. The python, suspicious, peeked with its triangular head and went right back inside when it saw the lion. The lion took a couple of steps back. Then it came out slowly, without taking its eyes off the cat. It slithered away to the ridge of a rock and stood in the sun while Jumbe watched it.

A few hours must have gone by in which the snake kept roaming among the rocks before a rodent entered one of the narrow cracks. The snake immediately sensed its arrival and prepared to attack. Camouflaged among the small stones, it closed the distance, but when it was within inches of reaching the naive visitor, the lion gave a little groan. The rodent instantly fled to seek refuge while the serpent bowed down understanding.

Throughout the day, there were several animals that dared to venture into the rock formation. Just one day before, all victims had died from snake venom. However, that day, all went their way. Each time the snake approached prey, the lion prevented the attack. Under these circumstances the serpent was compelled to take advantage of a previous victim to satisfy its hunger.

At dawn the next morning, Jumbe went to a second gap in the rock, where another snake still remained. Again, he repeated the operation he had used with the first nyoka. It spent the day observing how the lion forced its predecessor not to attack approaching animals. A few hours later, two snakes ended up eating the victims from the previous days, as Jumbe had done before. After the evening, he released three other snakes. All immediately went out looking for food. They had probably been thinking about his next prey for two days and nights, but when they left, they met two snakes eating prey that was already dead. They seemed to hesitate, but Jumbe, would block the road with a slight movement, and the accumulated hunger was enough to motivate them to join the others in their feast.

When the lion opened the sixth and seventh cracks in the rock, its occupants had such an appetite that they not even tried to find live prey. They followed the other's example and engulfed the former victims.

On the days that followed, the lion stood guard, but he did not have to trap them. When there was no more suitable food, Jumbe allowed attacking live animals, but only those necessary to satisfy their hunger and choosing the most vulnerable prey, those that sooner or later would have also fallen victims of other predators or environment accidents. Together, the snakes learned to leverage their efforts, so that if the prey would escape, another reptile was aware of it; and once satiated, they would retreat into their burrows to digest. Thus, more animals would dare to wander through the cracks in the rocks, and therefore, the food was more available. Soon, Jumbe did not have to intervene, and the snakes themselves regulated their hunting.

"It's a good story. It even made me hungry." I said gratefully. The man had managed to keep me entertained all morning.

"Certainly, it's time to eat and go." He said. "But before, I want to give you something to remember." Then, he introduced his hand in his red robe and pulled out a small wooden cube that he gave me. On one side he had drawn a snake and the inscription nyoka.

"Thanks." I said, welcoming the gift.

"I want you to think about the story I told and tell me five things that Jumbe did. Tomorrow will tell the story of twin leopards"

"Looks like another good story. I have only one question: What did you eat that day was in the rock?"

He smiled, showing his great and shiny teeth.

"A nomad knows how to find his food." He said, and left the room.

I spent all afternoon thinking about the story he had told me. I turned the small wooden cube around in my hand as if it were a puzzle. Of the six faces of the cube, only one was carved. The rest were blank, as if suggesting that I had to find those answers: five things that Jumbe had done; five things to dominate the snakes. The five faces of his behavior.

Mwalimu was clear that he wanted me to reflect on the story he had told me. My managerial mind began operating, and I remembered that Jumbe had reached the mountains and had found a group of snakes that were not effective. He had perceived their unproductive waste, since they ate many animals barely satisfied their needs, and that was an unsustainable model. Moreover, they seemed to go at it alone. Each one hunted and ate its own without worrying about what others did, even if there were leftovers. They even faced the lion. Jumbe had established a sustainable and useful order. But, how had he done it?

I asked the nurse to bring me a paper and pen and began to draw conclusions:

The first characteristic would be that Jumbe provided an efficient process that achieved results with the least expenses and ordered its compliance issuing mandatory instructions. He did not let the snakes anything but his orders until they saw they could succeed following this procedure.

To this end, a second characteristic was that his presence was continuous, and he did not lose sight of any of them and remained in place throughout the process.

A third issue would be that he controlled the snakes comprehensively and corrected them immediately. Thus instantly, he knew what they were doing right and wrong. In other words, he was establishing a rapid response control.

I kept trying to find the fourth one, covering the story in my head. Suddenly, I had the classic idea of rewards and punishments, because this imposes a prize or a punishment for each snake, depending on their behavior. It evaluates the result and not the individual.

I needed one more, the fifth one, and I remembered that all snakes were treated equally under the same rules. Only their individual behavior set them apart. That was, equal treatment.

I already had the five and the more I thought about it, the more I understood Jumbe's behavior towards the snakes. It was clear that the lion had understood the situation and knew how to handle it. "I could use my team!" I thought.

Then I wrote down five characteristics on paper:

- **The leader establishes an efficient procedure.**

- **He instructs mandatory rules.**

- **He provides a continuous presence.**

- **He establishes a rapid response control.**

- **He treats everyone equally.**

That night I slept with satisfaction that, despite being all day lying in bed, it had been a very useful day, and I began to wait impatiently for the story that Mwalimu had promised me the next day.

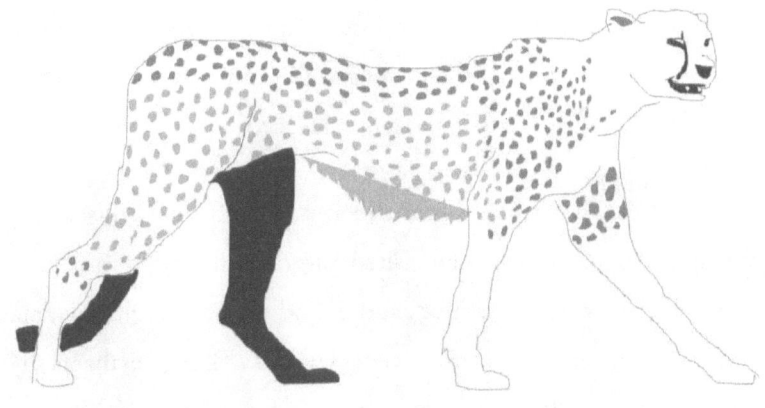

III.

The twin chuis

I admit I was glad to see Mwalimu at the door of the room an hour after breakfast. I could say that I did not have much to do, but the truth is that I was intrigued to know another story of the leader lion.

The first thing he did was ask me about my condition, which I thanked him, for although there was no change. My leg had to be immobilized for a while, the doctors wanted me to stay there for a few days to see how it responded after the surgery. Then he asked about the conclusions I had drawn from the history of the previous day, and I told him that I had written it in the notebook that the nurse had given me. He liked seeing that I had done my homework.

"Efficiency is very important for success. Few people can distinguish between effectiveness and efficiency. However, it is becoming increasingly important." He said.

"Yes, it is true." I remember once I explained this with a metaphor to a person that visited my department for the first time. We were in my office, and I said to him: "Differentiate between efficiency and effectiveness is easy. Imagine that a fly came into this office, and you want to kill it. You could blow up the office and end up finishing-off the fly... and the whole building. You would have been effective. However, you could also spray some insecticide into the air and the fly would die. You would have been effective and efficient." I told him.

We talked some more about the five characteristics of Jumbe's leadership that I had thought about and, eventually, I asked him directly if he was going to tell another story. He smiled. I guess I was expecting him to say it. So he continued his African story.

Jumbe left the rocks and went to the bush. Near a small stream, there was a limited grass field at the bottom of several elegant acacias. It was a beautiful place, and the sun lit up the horizon. It seemed to be shaking. Under the acacias, the freshness of the coveted shade gathered some animals. Our friend went there to relax, to lay in the grass that grew beside the trees.

His image conveyed serenity. I was able to focus on him, his calm face seemed to show consistently a slight smile. His body was formidable, powerful muscles accumulated beneath the sand color skin that looked like a soft velvet shawl tuck in a powerful machine. Around his head, small tufts of hair were beginning to grow, which soon would turn into a regal mane.

I do not know how long I was there enjoying the scenery. Several hours went by and then two leopards leaped out of nowhere. They were two young animals. I would say the same age. In fact, I've always thought of them as twins, and both were males. Although I have to admit that I use that description more to decorate the story.

The twins looked at Jumbe from a distance scrutinizing his intentions. One of them began to harass him, keeping ten or twenty yards away. Jumbe did not even pay attention. The leopard moved forward rapidly, and stopped in time to escape safely and issue a warning growl to the lion. On the third try, Jumbe looked at it straight. The leopard stopped immediately. This time he had stopped about 30 yards away. He could not even roar. Jumbe launched a huge roar that made all the birds in the area fly off the ground. Even I cringed, who had heard it at other times.

The leopard stepped back and ran with its partner. Jumbe did not even hint at getting up. However, he remained in the area enjoying the shade and the breeze that the acacias provided.

Occasionally, the two would run across the plain after each other. They ran all over while sprinting and twisting.. The view was magnificent. Sometimes their turns and hard braking were so sudden that they fell to the ground and raised a cloud of dry dust from which reappeared running at high speed. It was great to see the precision with which they moved. They had the speed that any animal would envy, including me.

By mid-afternoon a herd of gazelles, or paas, entered from the green horizon. As a very small army they marched in formation to the creek and then headed towards us.

The leopards stretched their necks to glimpse from afar, and sat on the grass, hugging the ground as close as possible. For a moment, they seemed to disappear in the horizontal line formed by dry foot-high vegetation. The naive gazelles continued to advance, not knowing what awaited them.

I have to admit that I was tempted to run to them to scare them away.

When at last the gazelles were close enough to get a glimpse of the predators, the leopards took off running suddenly at high speed. Their powerful legs, which had remained tense, stretched like springs that made them jump through the air. They ran so fast that I was difficult to tell when their claws rested on the ground. It seemed that they were flying right above the ground, shaking their bodies like a bow in the air.

Panic gripped the paas. None knew where to go. They were running and jumping to and fro, turning around and trying to find one another, and trying to see where the others were going, but they all did the same, and nobody made a decision, so they kept turning around in circles. The dust soon spread all over the place. The leopards entered the cloud. One paa got away and kept at a distance. However, most of the herd remained erratic in the cloud. Their heads or backs appeared and disappeared so that I could not count how many there were.

Suddenly, a cub emerged from the crowd followed by what seemed to be her mother. The leopards were fixed on her. Although it could run swiftly, it lacked the power of its mother. One of the leopards jumped on him, and its caregiver, in an instinctive reaction, try to block the leopard's path. However, the leopard dodged it and ran a few yards away from her. The offspring then felt so close to danger that it turned retracing its steps towards its mother. The maneuver had only delayed the leopard. Thus, the older gazelle directed its flight towards the herd, showing the offspring the road to follow. Perhaps, it was seeking the protection of the group or hoping the leopards chose another prey.

The twins followed them behind the dust cloud, and then I lost sight of them. Surprisingly, several panicked gazelles came out of the crowd. I expected to see one of the cats behind them, but the slender gazelles appeared scattered. Among them, there were the offspring and its mother.

There were more roaring and Jumbe joined in. For the first time, he was interested and that increased my curiosity even more. I strained to see what was happening. After a moment, a new figure was drawn in the dispersing dust. Behind the gazelles, or between them, a rhino appeared. The leopards, in pursuit, had encountered a tough opponent. Of course, they were quicker and more agile, but the strength of their opponent was greater.

Perhaps, motivated by their inexperience, or the thrill of the chase, one of them launched headlong into its head trying to grab his neck with his claws. The rhino, with little effort, lifted, turned and threw it several yards into the air. Seeing this, its comrade attacked in defense and found itself face to face with a unicorn skull. A dry sound stopped it in its attack, and it skidded to the ground. Only its agility and reflexes prevented it from perishing trampled under the heavy ruminant.

Jumbe watched the scene as he approached slowly. The leopards fell, wounded, to recover. They remained a few seconds looking at each other, while kept an eye on the rhino and the lion, which was very close. It seemed they were talking to each other. It was clear they were not winning that battle.

40

Then they threw themselves at the same time against the formidable animal. I believe, they did that sue to their youthful wounded pride and thoughtlessness; it was clear he was not a prey for them. The result was no different. In an onslaught, they flew several yards away, landing badly wounded on the ground. The rhino was not happy, and attacked them. At that time Jumbe lurched at the rhino. I feared that he would receive a blow similar to the one the leopards had suffered. However, when the lion was heading straight toward the animal, he made turned at the last moment, dodged its formidable horn and flipped on a single jump, and landed a blow on the rhino's hind. The rhino lost balance trying to hit the lion with its head, and not being able to bear the blow, it landed on the ground.

Beaten, with half its back on the sand, it gave a snort of rage and tried to get up immediately, but the lion jumped on its head, and the rhino ended lying on the plain. He then broke away quietly, with an air of satisfaction. The rhino, strangely, seemed to hesitate, but again got up drawing strength from its anger. The lion looked at it and looked at the leopards, who understood his message: he was letting them take a turn.

The rhino was not willing to play that game, so it ran toward them; they separated and dodged just before being struck. With the lesson learned, one of the cats ran into the back and hit it, rendering making the rhino lose its balance. The second leopard topped that with another lateral collision. The rhino was back on the floor.

Both cats surrounded the rhino, running with agile movements. They were proud and enjoying that success.

Only that Jumbe's roar prevented attacking the rhino, which rested, tired, on the ground. The lion was not willing to give them the kill. Both understood and retreated under the acacias. The rhino also understood and got up to go away.

The leopards spent the rest of the day with the lion. They looked with awe and reverence, and he even allowed them to share with him an old gazelle that he had hunted that afternoon."

I was not aware of how much time had gone by, so was surprised when a nurse appeared with lunch. It seemed as if Mwalimu had measured the story to complete it right on time.

"Well, it's time to eat, like Jumbe and the chui." He said as he placed \his hand in his robe to extract another wooden cube.

On this occasion, he gave me a wooden cube of equal size, color and shape as the one before, except that now, on one of its faces, two leopards were drawn. The nurse looked at his gesture curiously while the cubes remained on the white side table that was next to the bed. Mwalimu then politely said goodbye and left.

Again, I spent the afternoon trying to define five conclusions from the story I was told. In the book placed on the plaster on my leg, I wrote my thoughts on what Jumbe had done with the leopards.

In my opinion, firstly, Jumbe had demanded respect and had controlled from a distance the behavior of the agile felines. He had left them stumble and wander before acting. He kept his power over them, while they had made mistakes.

Another thing that struck me is that, eventually, he defended them before the rhino. It is important that a leader is able to stand up for his own and become a hero and protector in their eyes.

He is also a role model, his behavior serves as an example, and he teaches them and transfers his own knowledge.

Then he demanded that they do the same. He was able to overcome the rhino, but also they to repeat the feat. Thus, he had found that they were trained. He achieved to have them perform on their own because he was there for them, in case they failed.

And finally, a behavior that I too would like to use: he shared the prize with them. He is not a lone leader staying away from his team, but a leader who remains nearby and celebrates the successes together.

Now, I was satisfied with the story. The fact that I reviewed what Mwalimu told me, was slowly opening my eyes. The more I thought about it, the more similarities I found was with my career. Now, I was thinking about the snakes and leopards that I had met at different times. And I was wondering what the next animal was.

And this is what I wrote in my notebook:

• **The leader demands respect and controls from a distance.**

• **Eventually, he defends the team.**

• **He is a role model, his behavior is an example, and he teaches and transmits.**

• **He ensures that the team is trained.**

• **He shares success.**

IV.

The passage of tumbulis

When Mwalimu arrived, I had prepared a surprise. Upon entering the room my bed was empty, and he was stunned. I watched the scene from a corner, from my brand new wheelchair provided by the hospital.

"Good morning." I said in order to prevent surprise to from causing for concern.

"Good morning." He said, smiling with the sincerity of those who really are glad to see someone again.

"Today we leave this room. They told me that there is a large terrace where we can stay until lunch," I suggested.

"That is a great idea. The fresh air will do you good." He said.

On the terrace the views were extraordinary. It was oriented to the south of the hospital, just on the opposite side of the entrance and the road to the city. Behind the building you could see a beautiful hill with a lot of vegetation. At its peak, a small veranda and a white sculpture were illuminated by the sun. But what I enjoyed most was the aroma. I had spent several days holed up in that hospital room that smelled of disinfectant, and the smell of clean air and the countryside reminded me of the importance of a good environment. I remembered the number of times that I had corrected some managers when I visited the branches and found boxes and dirt on them.

Mwalimu also enjoyed the scenery. He noted the veranda at the top of the mountain and told me it had a special meaning, for there, once the mfalme or king of the tribe climbed to seek advice.

"When you're leading, heights are dangerous." He said. "I have seen many mfalme making mistakes as a result of going up there seeking advice. From the top, things look very different. Sometimes that is good, but sometimes is very bad. You have to know how to be at the two levels and not see things only from above.

"You are very right." I said crestfallen.

"When you ask others to go up the road; in other words, when you ask others to make an effort, you must realize that from above it seems that the road is downhill, but those who are at the foot of the mountain see it going up. Therefore, it is important that they not always see you on top, but make them understand that they are able to climb up the road.

"I understand, but sometimes you do not have time to do demonstrations." I said.

"You don't need them. They must think we're capable of doing it; although we have not yet come to that story. Today I'll tell you one that happened back in the mountains."

"After meeting the leopards, Jumbe stayed for some time with them in the bush, so I returned to my home. Weeks later someone told me that he had seen the lion again in the mountains and curiosity took me to him. After the mountains, at the end of the roads and shortcuts, where the snakes do not reach, there is a large ridge that cuts off the path. Dozens of vervet monkeys live there or as we call in our language, tumbulis, organized into several families. The place looked like a wasteland. Where once there seemed to be vegetation, now there were dead trees and bare weeds. It was like a big bald spot on the mountain. I thought that this was due to the monkeys' exploitation. Many, for so long, enclosed between the ridge and the nyoka who waited below, had consumed all food sources.

Jumbe was still there in the center, lying. I do not know how long he was there. The monkeys watched from afar, grouped in small families. All of them looked like starving animals, emaciated face, and slow movements. Normally, tumbulis tend to be restless animals, difficult to contain. However, those animals were passive and fearful. They looked at each other hoping that one of them would take the first step, but no one dared. Jumbe, as always, was examining the situation carefully. He seemed glad to see me, and I was watching until I settled on top of a small rock formation. At that time, the show started.

The lion got up with great agility, took a couple of jumps and began to stalk each of the families. At first I thought he was going to attack, but actually he approached at high speed towards them, and when he had reached them and could touch them, jumped into another family to repeat the same operation. He moved this way across the area as if he wanted to introduce himself to each family. The monkeys, unable to flee or defend themselves, came together more and more. At one point, all the families were gathered in one place. Then I realized, he was herding them like we herd cows and grouping them to confine them.

At that very instant, Jumbe stopped short and drew in the watchful eyes of all monkeys. It was like when an artist brings to the tourists in the streets of Dar es Salaam to play his show. He had finally attracted their attention and was preparing to offer his. Jumbe raised his face to the sky and roared and immediately we were all mesmerized by his presence. He looked at us and ran back to the side while their eyes followed him. He ran and ran toward the rift that cut through the mountain, and as he ran, I was increasingly holding my breath. I cringed in fear that he was going to be launched into the air. That possibility had not even remotely entered my mind, but that seemed to be his intention. The lion reached the rift and disappeared into the air. We were all absorbed. Before our eyes, a young lion, with a whole life ahead, had pulled in a mad rush and had thrown himself off a cliff. I could not believe what I had just witnessed. The tumbulis and I had been so surprised that there was silence for a few seconds giving the place an eerie air.

Suddenly, down the road, at the horizontal line where Jumbe had disappeared, which separated the sky from the rugged terrain, he reappeared with a big jump. As if it had been choreographed, the tumbulis drew back together, and right after, they opened their mouths as they stared in surprise. The lion roared again, and when we all looked, he stepped back and disappeared again.

This time everyone gave several steps forward to try to look at his fall. First, quickly, then, the closer we got, slower. When some tumbulis were just about three yards from the ravine, Jumbe jumped up suddenly and made them fall to the ground in shock. However, he made no move to attack. He just simply moved away to the side to let them look. Little by little, afraid of falling and for the cat, the monkeys were approaching, glued to the ground. There, they looked out, stayed a while examining what they saw. For a moment they forgot all that at their side, next to them, there was a lion. Then, Jumbe jumped again above them. About two yards below a rock protruding from the vertical wall that descended to the ground stopped his fall. The tumbulis were surprised to see Jumbe falling before their eyes, but still continued to look. I, gradually, managed to find a good position where I could watch them from.

The lion looked up again and his eyes met those of the tumbulis and mine. When he made sure that we kept watching him, he jumped again, this time to another rock about two yards below. This was a strange sight, because he would move sharply away from us and his figure was dwarfed by the landscape offered by the greenery of the canyon. We were looking for a while at the figure, until he roared towards us. A young monkey dropped slowly sliding down to the rock where the cat previously was standing. At the same moment, Jumbe gave a new leap towards a projecting rock further away. Everyone looked amazed.

Another roar prompted the monkey to drop to the second step on the improvised ladder the lion was making. A second roar made another tumbuli falls to the first step. At the same time, Jumbe dropped into another rock and I lost sight of him, as it was right about five or six feet below the first one on which he jumped. His followers repeated the process, each occupying the next step. Soon all the monkeys were on a rock down the mountainside.

It took me a few seconds to think about it, because the height was considerable, but I was a young boy, and my more curiosity pulled me more than my fear, so I jumped in pursuit. I have to admit that, years later, I went there to show a tourist the landscape and I surprised by having been capable to do this madness. Somehow, I came down with them following them from rock to rock, jump to jump, risking my life with each jump until finally reaching the ground.

The monkeys were running around like crazy and scattering among the weeds. It was a totally different place from the top. Though the river, which many generations ago had created the canyon, did not exist anymore, there was something left of it beneath our feet, since many bushes and trees were growing there. Jumbe was sitting on his haunches and watched with joy the enjoyment of the tumbulis. Infected by them, I ran to the small field of fresh grass, next to a group of trees, like an animal. When I was halfway I discovered Jumbe jumping beside me, as if with me. However, I did not fear anything. At that moment, I understood that we were friends.

The monkeys watched us from the various points where they were, and they changed their direction to follow us. Everyone jumped, ran, we threw ourselves to the ground and got up again in the grass. Some tumbulis climbed up the trees and picked up some fruit, throwing it to those below. I laid on the floor overflowing with joy and exhaustion. I was exhausted. It was very nice to have achieved that success. I had to gather my breath, which took a few minutes, and then I sat on the floor to see the others: the tumbulis were clustered eating fruit along a tree log. On the other side, Jumbe was lying down and watched it all. Behind me, the great mountain showed me the madness we had just gone through. A vertical wall of bare rock rose about a couple of hundred feet above the ground. The sun rays lit up mercilessly making the view even harder. I struggled to identify the path that we followed, but I was unable to distinguish further than six steps. I spent a while trying different routes, but on reaching the sixth projection, the jumps seemed too distant for me to have achieved them. No doubt, none could have done that feat if it were not for Jumbe."

I was so taken by the story that when he finished, I discovered that his hands held a third piece of wood of equal size and shape as those adorning my side table. On one side he had drawn the outline of a monkey climbing.

This time, I was prepared. While Mwalimu told the story I had been thinking about the actions that Jumbe performed and had outlined some ideas in the notebook. So, when he gave me the third piece of wood, I suggested summarizing the five most important actions that Jumbe had achieved and he agreed.

The first thing I had noticed was that Jumbe, to reach the top of the cliff, introduced himself to the monkeys ostentatiously. With the snakes and the leopards, at first, he had gone unnoticed until it was time to take action.

In this case, he made himself noted directly and became a role model for the monkeys.

Then, once he made sure we all watched, he began to lead by example, doing things so that everyone would be clear on what to do.

Therefore, to them he was playing the leading role on what to do. He did not order anyone, or made them accompany him, but he acts alone. They say a picture is worth a thousand words; thus, Jumbe had shown the way forward.

Of course this does not work if the goal is not reached. Jumbe got results one by one and asked others for achieving before continuing to the next. He was patient and did not demand all to those who did not know how to get it, but teaches the tasks in sections, one at a time, until it was fulfilled.

In other words, he ensures that they achieved the result and monitored the actions of those who follow him. In this way, he reinforced the correct behavior of his collaborators, because they felt confident by having him as a role model and possible help, and he made sure they had understood.

"Okay, I see that you have been paying attention to my story." He congratulated me after hearing my speech. "You have realized that Jumbe's priority was to teach the monkeys. In the case of the snakes he had to teach the correct behavior, but also had to unite them, and also got them to follow his orders. He had to teach the leopards and got them to accept him, because they were already united. In this case, the monkeys accepted his instructions, but they needed someone to unite them and teach them as a role model, a guide. You see, Jumbe's behavior was an outline. When I finish to tell you the stories, you will understand and they will help you in leading your business. Now I must go to rest, tomorrow we will continue." Said Mwalimu, and left me waiting to see him the next day.

This is what I wrote about the story of Jumbe and the monkeys:

• The leader becomes the role model for the team.

• He gives an example so that everyone knows what to do.

• He becomes the lead player.

• He gets the results one by one.

• He makes sure the team achieves the results and monitors.

V.

The bored kongonis

The next morning, Mwalimu came a little later and that worried me. I feared not seeing him again because he was tired of visiting me, or other occupation had taken him away from me. Nothing was further from the truth. The truth is that Mwalimu had gone to pick up another person who accompanied him when he showed up in my room.

Sir John Bald was a big man, about 50 years old, with white hair and sun-beaten skin. He was wearing a safari outfit. Although, in this region, his wardrobe did not indicate his

56

occupation, which in this case was precisely being a guide, tracker and hunter.

The three went down to the terrace and we were talking about the world and its problems for a while. Sir John had lived in Africa since his childhood. His father had fought against the Desert Fox in the battle of El Alamein during the Second World War under Montgomery's command, and several years after the war, he agreed to serve in an embassy. So Sir John came to Africa when he was nine years old and had spent more than four decades in the continent. First, he served in the British army, where he reached a high rank, then he succeeded his father at the Embassy and, when he retired from active duty, he chose to work with animals. Currently, he was heading a reservation a few miles from Morogoro and a photographic safari tour guide company. Precisely, the one my travel agency had hired and where Mbuto worked.

Mwalimu told me that Sir John had asked about my condition every day since I suffered the accident and had asked several times to accompany him. So this morning before going to the hospital, Mwalimu went to pick him up.

"Besides, I would like that Sir John tell us the story he experienced together with Jumbe." said Mwalimu.

"It will be a pleasure." said the Briton. "It happened two years ago in the south, near Mtwara. I had already left the embassy and was preparing for a game reserve in a large estate donated by the government. I traveled the country looking for all kinds of animals. In the reserve, we had two families of elephants, but we needed to create an ecosystem that would support the most important native animals.

In Kebasa, near the Ruvuma River, I drove my jeep looking for large herbivores. I followed the river until I found a large esplanade and camped for a day. At dawn, I awoke startled feeling the earth move under my body. That really seemed like an earthquake, but when I stepped out of my tent, I saw that a huge herd of wildebeest slowly approached the river." The kongonis or nyumbus, as they are known around here, are large animals like bison, which tend to cluster in large herds. The magnitude was such that the whole floor vibrated as they moved.

The kongonis marched slowly moving their tails up and down and looking at the ground that preceded them. They followed each other without even looking at the scenery. Rather than on their way to eat, they seemed they were doing penance.

It was a time when I was quite sensitive, since my recent retirement had left me somewhat depressed. So, I recognized myself when I saw them. They seemed to have no desire for anything. They moved without knowing why, following each other."

"Yes, I've seen things like that at the assembly line. They are there but nobody is home." I said, unable to remain silent.

"Yes, it is true." "The wildebeest acted instinctively, repeating their past but meaningless behaviors. Soon, the field was almost overrun by animals, moving like a big shapeless gray mass. Their wandering, uniform and weary, took to the river, where they began drinking. The first ones took positions, and lowering their nose to the bank, began to suck slowing the whole herd that followed. The rest met up with them and, for a moment, failed to react. Forced by the pushing and shoving, some of the heads in front plunged in the river, making room for others to reach it. Others took to the sides until they reached the water. Still, there were so many animals left behind bellowing without a response. Nobody seemed to listen. If they reached the water, they did not care about the others.

Then Jumbe appeared in the horizon. I remember that scene because I felt we were similar. We both looked at the kongonis, each at one end. The lion was studying the movements of the gnus. I thought he was planning how to attack them, but I was wrong.

A loud roar announced his arrival; however, the kongonis were so many and so loud, and so busy pushing and resisting the push of others, that only a few of them barely heard the roar. Jumbe came down the small hill that separated him from them increasing the speed with each stride. When he was close, he started to galloping like it was a hunting day. He reached sufficient speed and jumped about two feet into the river, where the depth was still minimal. Jumping and roaring, he ran along the bank and at times, dodged some kongonis that were drinking and had not been able to move away. As soon as they noted his presence, the direction of the pushing was directed to the opposite side. Now everyone wanted to get away from the water. He spent several minutes growling and threatening those who came to the water until they froze in front of the, at about three to six feet away.

It was an incredible situation, and I was a witness. I can assure you that if I had carried a camera, the images would have made it around the world. The lion was in the river, with his paws immersed in water. Had taken a stern pose; he was holding up his face and standing firmly on his feet. His roars silenced the kongonis herd. On the left, dozens of them bunched together in silence. Most tried to observe the lion, while some were hidden behind the spines of others. Between the lion and them, there was a five-foot aisle.

Then Jumbe launched towards the right flank of the kongonis. Right after, the pack split; some went to one side and the rest to the other. Running through the gap formed between the two groups of frightened wildebeests, he reached the rear of the herd and immediately turned to the right. The few who had separated from the rest of the herd were pushed by the lion, which was coming from behind towards the water making threatening noises. In just two or three seconds a part of the herd had entered the river, while the rest remained on land in expectation. Jumbe turned his back to them, making sure that none of the rest of the flock would follow him. After a moment of amazement, they realized that the lion would not attack and began drinking.

After a few minutes, some kongonis came out of the water slowly, afraid of being attacked. But Jumbe turned and roared to those who still remained in, and they came out quickly.

Once no kongoni remained in the water, he ran back towards the left flank, separated a small group and took them to the water.

The process was repeated several times, until all the wildebeests had the opportunity to drink. When finished, Jumbe quenched his thirst and went up the same hill from which he had appeared.

That lesson was not forgotten because since then, that herd always turns to drink.

The rest of the day the gnus were kept in the esplanade, opposite to the current. Jumbe returned the next day, but the kongonis did not receive him with fear but with awe. They all looked at him and those who were lying on the floor stood up to watch. The lion stood in the middle of the hill, where everyone could see him, and watched them all, from left to right and front to back. We all waited to see what he was doing.

He stood on his hind legs and let out a huge roar. It was an image I've seen in many coats of arms, as those in Windsor Castle, the image of a rampant lion. He then slowly turned and walked slowly up the hill. All kongoni were prompted to follow and see where he went. At one point, his image faded into the horizon and the kongonis began to ascend the hill. I hopped into the jeep and started the engine. I did not want to miss the show.

From a distance, I followed the herd for several miles. At first, I was parallel to the flow of the river, but after a few hundred yards, we separated to surround a rock formation. We continued through a clump of trees and bushes, and finally, climbed up a new hill without problems. From its summit, one could see a beautiful landscape. A huge space that seemed endless and merged with the sky stretched out before my eyes. It was as if I had shrunk and was on top of a map. I could clearly distinguish several groups of trees, mostly acacias, some animals scattered around the area, elephants, leopards, giraffes and, best of all, in the center as a meeting place for all of them, a large lagoon.

They left in that direction and Jumbe backed away from the head of the heard and mingled among the buffalo, because they already knew the road. The kongonis changed their nature completely. If before, they were slow, noisy, looked down and let

62

the herd carry them around, now, they were running around in small groups into the lagoon. On arrival to the water they enjoyed together, playing and jumping in it. Jumbe looked like a member of the pack instead of a predator.

"Wow, it's a fantastic story, but I guess that you missed the opportunity to get animals for your park," I cried.

"No. In fact, I took them and this is the largest group of animals that we have there." He said.

"Really?" I asked, surprised. I do not understand how he could do if they had that wonderful place. I guess he had to force them.

"No, nothing like that; I never wanted to force animals to live on the reservation. In this case, it was simple, it was something Jumbe decided; he went to the reservation and the others followed." He answered.

"I knew you'd like your story." Mwalimu stood up and helped me to do likewise. We went to my room slowly.

"But if you want to get another cube, you should tell John and me five conclusions from Jumbe's behavior." He said, jokingly, with a piece of wood in his hand.

"Opps, I will," I replied. The truth is I was so amused by the story that I had forgotten that the Guru was present.

Once in the room, I took out my notebook, which remained on the table, under the three pieces of wood that he had given me earlier. I held it with my left hand while moving away the cubes and picked up the pen with the right hand. I opened the notebook to the next page and began my explanation:

"When Jumbe saw the kongonis arriving, he realizes that they do not act well, they don't know what to do. So first of all, he showed them how to do tasks well or how to improve them. He separated them to teach them how to turn in the river, so everyone can drink."

"Well, I've noticed that in this case the kongonis are united and accept Jumbe's orders. That is why he focuses on improving their capabilities." Said Mwalimu while John Bald watched him.

"Right. But that was not enough for Jumbe. The kongonis needed something more than learning what to do. They had lost their enthusiasm. They lacked joy. So the second behavior that Jumbe taught was to innovate and discover things, showing them a new path. This leads us to a third characteristic, which is to present a vision, a future with enthusiasm. When he led them through trees and bushes and they climbed the hill with him, everyone could see the great lake, the positive future that awaits them. Jumbe is a visionary leader who must motivate his followers," I continued.

"Indeed, I have seen this in the military. True leaders say more with body language than with the content of their messages. Everyone is aware of them and it is crucial that they show enthusiasm. There is nothing worse than going to work and seeing your boss unmotivated." "Motivation is the most contagious felling in an organization," added the Englishman.

"Sure." I said enthusiastically; perhaps trying to prevent them from thinking that I was one of those sad bosses. Jumbe not only guided them, transmitting his energy to the others, but actually celebrated and enjoyed the success publicly and notoriously. He made they reach their goal and then joined in the celebration to show that success had been achieved. So he showed the path to success clearly marked. Finally, there is a fifth characteristic, which is to stay attentive to each other's relations, creating team synergy and avoiding any differences. When boredom arises in a team, conflicts may arise and a good leader must ensure they do not happen anymore."

"Great. I see you have understood the story and also been infected by Jumbe's energy. Laziness, boredom, and lack of motivation are great enemies of organizations today, but remember that imagination is energy capable of achieving great things. This imagination is like the light bulb and the bulb must be the leader." Said Mwalimu while he was handing me a new wooden cube.

"Thank you. I couldn't agree more. The leader is a catalyst of energy. He must be able to produce it, announce it and capture it to illuminate his team. That reminds me of a phrase attributed to the scientist Albert Einstein: 'There is a driving force more powerful than steam, electricity and nuclear power: willpower,'" I recited, trying to show off as a scholar.

"Absolutely. Well, I think the talk today was a very interesting, but we must leave. Remember that you must rest." Mwalimu said goodbye, leaving me with the mystery of knowing the contents of the Jumbe's next adventure.

This is what wrote that day on my notebook:

- **The leader shows how to do tasks well, how to improve themselves.**
- **The leader innovates; discovers new things to others.**
- **Enthusiastically, he presents a vision, a future.**
- **He celebrates and enjoys success, publicly and notoriously.**
- **He creates team synergy and avoids any differences.**

VI.

The team of mambas

I had become used to going down in the morning, with my notebook under my arm, to the terrace in order to meet Mwalimu. There he was, looking at the sky surrounding the hilltop. It was a blue undisturbed sky. There was no trace of any clouds. Then he turned toward me and I noticed in his face signs of restlessness.

"Worried about rain?" I asked, knowing the answer.

"Yes. My people need the fields to bear fruit. There were not rain in many days. The dry season being longer than ever"

"Maybe you should think of ways to store water during the rainy season or something like that." Said my engineer's mind.

"Yes, but it's hard. Here, the rain governs everything, and is not easily manageable. When it rains, it does overwhelmingly, and when it does not, it is for too long. Today will tell a story about our lion and rain.

The past rainy season began, as always, unexpectedly. One day as clear as today, gave way the next morning; it rained for three continuously, so strongly that the raindrops could not be distinguished. The horizon was covered by a wall of rain coming down steadily.

The channels of ancient rivers unknown to me, filled with currents that dragged everything in their path. The Rufiji River, which flows from the lands of Dodoma to the coast, opposite the island of Mafia, had remained until then a small volume, enough to attract many animals to its banks. During the dry season, animals throughout the region had survived thanks to it and had settled on the prairies around it.

I was following Jumbe at the bottom of the river, accompanied by a family of elephants and a herd of kongonis. I remember that I had to improvise a bed of mpingo leaves and branches to keep moisture out. The rain never stopped falling on the plain and the river level was high, two or three yards wider than normal.

When the rains ceased, three days later, it was as if suddenly silence reigned. Then the animals regained their vitality and began their usual chores.

Two days later, the river level lowered. I thought that everything was back to normal, but the strange thing was that it continued lowering until it became virtually dry.

Jumbe, who had been watching the river several times, circled the animals worried. I think he was checking the condition of each and every one of them. When finished, he ascended the river to its source. And, of course, I picked up the few clothes I had and got ready to accompany him.

I walked about twenty yards behind him for miles, and found that every minute the river level was going down more and more. A day away, we discovered the cause.

On the riverbed, a log, probably driven by the great flood of the previous days, was trapped side to side on the river. The two ends had been engaged in the mud on both sides and the force of water had partially buried it. The steady stream had accumulated over many branches, sediment and even stones, forming a natural dam.

We continued unit we surpass it. Behind, a natural lagoon had formed which exceeded the bed and was flooding the plain. Several animals that lived in the area or who, like us, had come in search of water, were enjoying it without effort. But that concentration of animals also attracted predators.

As I watched a wildebeest stretching its neck to place its tong in the water, I noticed that a few inches away, a crocodile, a mamba, remained hidden in the mud. When it launched its sudden attack, I jumped back, startled in fright. The crocodile had been trapped the kongoni's neck in its jaws and dragged it toward the center of river. The animal kicked and tried to pull, but it soon became submerged and its movements slowly turned-off like the flame of a candle.

Instinctively, I looked around for hidden mambas close by, but fortunately they were focusing on bulkier prey. I counted four crocodiles in different stretches of the river: three on this side and another on the opposite side. Each acted independently to capture prey.

The first, the largest, measured more than five yards and its enormous power had been able to immobilize the wildebeest.

Ten or twelve yards above another much smaller crocodile devoured a lightweight wading bird that had just flown in. It had captured it thanks to a well-aimed blow of its slender tail, which it handled with skill.

70

Facing it across the river, a third reptile running at high speed after a rodent which mistakenly thought it was faster than a crocodile.

In the middle of the river, a fourth crocodile displayed a huge fish in his teeth that was caught swimming upstream.

It was certainly an idyllic situation for them. All animals approached the water without objection and they only had to wait.

Jumbe roared like thunder and made everyone turn, even the crocodiles that were so busy. As soon as he caught their attention, he ran to makeshift dike, knowing that was the target of our gaze. He jumped up and walked to the center of the river. The water level continued to rise while more debris piled next to the log. Jumbe sank one of his claws and pulled it out. Immediately, I realized that he was trying to show that water was likely to bring down the dam and the force would drag them down too.

The fourth crocodile, which was in the water, went to the log and swam from one end to another. Then it stayed on the right side and pushed hard. The dam did not budge. Jumbe ran back to the bank and approached the first crocodile, which stood beside the corpse of the wildebeest. It was nearly three yards larger than the lion, for a moment, I feared it would attack him. Jumbe must have thought the same thing, because he jumped around to prevent the attack. The huge reptile, with a good kill in its mouth, did not seem to want to risk a fight with the cat; especially without the advantage of surprise. Jumbe harassed and instigated it by showing his powerful teeth and even threatened it with swipe in the weakest point of the crocodiles, their eyes. Lazily, the crocodile came out of the river pushed by Jumbe, who led it to the dam.

Now, two were pushing, but the log did not move.

Again, he ran for a third crocodile. This time he chose the one with wiggle its tail in the air as it approached others. The fourth mamba ran toward them attracted by curiosity.

Jumbe pointed the third crocodile a hole in the log that had been plugged by mud carried by the water. The mamba whipped it with his tail and the mud fell off. The water pressure pushed a penetrating jet, and by accessing the other side, it began its descent at high speed. In the lagoon there was a big current that trapped several fish and threw them into the hole, leaving them lifeless, prostrated before them on the dry side.

Seeing that scene, the four crocodiles realized that they could suffer the same fate and began to push with all their might. However, the log did not move an inch. Jumbe roared and they stopped. With a nod, he ordered the first crocodile to the dry side and placed it on the left side of the log. He made the third one climb on the right side next to the second, and made the fourth climb with him on the log.

When they all were in their places, he roared again. On the left side, the big crocodile pushed the log to the water in the direction opposite to the current; at the other end, two crocodiles pushed down. Jumbe and the fourth crocodile spun the log with their feet; little by little, the mud fell off the surface. When it turned, water penetrated below it and lifted it just enough so they could move it. As they all pushed in different directions, the log began to rotate horizontally.

When the right end gave, it opened a few inches for water to pass; the current pushed so that the two crocodiles had to get out to the side of the river. The water created a gap between the log and the sediment and moments later the log turned completely. The large crocodile received a slap of water that pushed it inland. At high speed, Jumbe and the crocodiles that were on the log ran to the bank just as it turned. The six of us stood watching the log descending downstream.

Jumbe roared and crocodiles looked at him from where they were. I could see in their eyes the satisfaction of accomplishment.

The river had returned to normal and ran to the mouth quickly. The fish kept jumping for a few moments into the air. The animals, hearing the sound of running water, happily approached the river bank. I could watch the scene from a few miles below. After an extreme drought, they were now enjoying a fresh water spring that would satisfy their thirst and would water the plants that serve as food.

It was one of the most extraordinary moments of my life. I felt that the life of those animals was meant only for that performance.

Well, I think that's enough. This story must have shown you other qualities of a leader." He concluded, handing me a new piece of wood.

"Of course. It was very interesting." I said.

"Great! As we now ran out of time, and I see that you noted down several things in your notebook, how about if we talk about the five characteristics that the story showed you?" He asked politely.

"Sure, of course." I said, although I had doubts. The first one is that the leader sees beyond his team. He has a vision that goes beyond his scope of work and examines the consequences in other areas and for the future.

"Yes, it is true." "Jumbe goes beyond the place where his team is and realizes the consequences of water not reaching downstream. A department head must be aware of the meaning of his team's work in the final result. It's like the department head who knows the functions and duties of departments related to him and thus can help establishing improvements for his team to be more efficient." Said Mwalimu, who wanted me to see the similarity this had with my business.

"Another characteristic," I continued, "would be to communicate that vision to the team for them to see its importance. It is one of the main forms of motivation. I have always believed that people like to know what their job means to the company. I remember a little story that I heard in a motivational seminar in which a medieval knight finds a child carrying a stone to the mountain and asks what he is doing. The boy replied that he was forced to carry a rock all his life because he was an inferior being and his life was a punishment. Then the knight pulled the boy up on his horse and took him miles ahead, where a huge cathedral was being built with the rocks from the mountain. He showed him that monument, introduced him to the builder, who showed him the drawings and explained that it was the most important cathedral in history and that they were building it as a tribute to God. The child, of course, took back the rock, but since then he had a reason to do so, and he did not think of himself as inferior or felt he had been punished."

"Okay. It is also a great story." - He approved.

"Thirdly, for the true leader, what motivates the team is not a person, but the mission and the objective pursued. At first they did not pay attention to Jumbe, but when the crocodiles saw the importance of their mission, they put themselves to work quickly. It is very important to be able to tell the team members what is the work to be performed, the expected results and the reward." I said firmly.

"Yes, it is true." People need to keep things clear. Insecurity is not good and uncertainty." Answered Mwalimu

Another important aspect is that the leader is able to detect the strengths and weaknesses of team members. In addition, he must give each a role within the team, and show them the importance of their work to achieve the goal. It's like the team coach who places players in the right places. Each one is better in one place or another." I explained, reading my book.

"Of course. And remember that the team coach often is not necessarily the best player. Rarely, a basketball team coach is the tallest or the best shooter." He said, and gestured as if shooting a ball into the hoop.

"Finally, he participates in the team's actions and gets involved, but allows each one do his job. Jumbe is there for them and intervenes only to lend a hand when he sees the need," and so I wrote in the notebook.

"Okay. I could not have done it better." He complimented with a wide grin as he showed me a piece of wood with a crocodile drawn on one side. "Without doubt, you deserve to run your business. I think you have won a prize. It's okay for today. Tomorrow we'll meet again." He said, and left.

This is what I wrote in the book:

• **The leader has a vision that goes beyond his scope of work.**

• **He communicates that vision to the team to be aware of its importance.**

• **What motivates the team is not a person but the mission and the objective pursued.**

• **The leader must be able to identify the strengths and weaknesses of the team members.**

• **He participates in the team's activities and gets involved, but he allows everyone to do their job.**

VII.

The four fisis

That morning, I received two calls. The first on was from Lydia, the human resources director. Apparently, they had a hard time reaching me after receiving the news of my accident from the travel agency. Of course, she offered me all kinds of help from her department, which I refused politely. The truth is that little could be done. Three days were left before the return flight and it did not make much sense to cancel it and raise the trip's costs. I was no worse off there than in any other hospital and I had was really relaxing.

Minutes later Jack, the President called, who was enjoying his vacation in Spain. I was used to talk about serious issues with him, but that was a very different conversation. We talked for a good time about vacations and the need to take them. Certainly, the routine and pace of work is often hide us from the right direction and even the landscape. When we stop, we can think about what we do and, in most cases, we find ways to make things better. Talking with him about inconsequential issues in the workplace as we used I found in him a person unknown to me. Outside the company he had his family and hobbies. He made me see that during the holidays, he focused on giving quality time to his family. I felt I barely knew him and I wondered what I colleagues would see in me. I spent a long time reviewing their work, their skills and capabilities, but never allowed them to give me their opinion about me.

As a good leader, I was confident of my abilities, so confident that I would never allow it to be questioned. At that point, I decided that when I returned, I would make each and every one of them examine me. It would be a starting point to get to lead them, that is, first he must be able to lead myself.

Moreover, the hospital continued to maintain its protocols. After eating the sterile breakfast, I walked to the balcony to talk to Mwalimu. I liked to spend time with him; I would pass the time, and my thinking was motivated at the same time. His stories were much deeper when I meditated on them in the afternoon. In fact, the notebook in which I took notes from his stories had become my best companion in the evenings.

Mwalimu arrived shortly after and talked about the conversation I had with my boss. He agreed on the need to know oneself in order to improve. I explained that we often think that we are so good that we need no improvement. And he answered:

"Many years ago the village chief had a horse. Few people here have a horse, so horse owners know each other well. It is a mark of distinction and power. Each year, they used to met and race them. The horse that belonged to this chief was the best. Every year, he used to win the race and that made him proud. He looked after and pampered that animal all year long waiting for the day when he could return to win the race. However, every year there were fewer competitors. This made him feel even more important, thinking that they dared not face his animal. A couple of years later he was invited to a tournament and prepared thoroughly his horse. When he arrived, all the participants looked at him amazed and began to whisper in fun. All those who had been one time or another defeated had come this time. He thought it was a great day to demonstrate the agility of his beloved animal. But when he went to the race track, he discovered that only he had brought a horse. All the chiefs, rich people and landowners of the area had invested in brand new SUVs. Of course, he still had the best horse, but the competition had changed. All others, aware of their weaknesses, had sought innovative solutions. He, who does not discover his weakness, ends up just being overcome by it."

That story reminded me that Jumbe had left a family to seek his destiny, so I asked about it.

"I see you listen closely." He said gratefully. "Jumbe reunited with his family. In the dry season, the lion was roaming through the meadow in the distance when he saw his former mates, his family.

Jumbe longed to meet them, but was did not run to join them. With them was Kun, the leader who months earlier had expelled him. He was able to see his mother, his sisters and his lazy playmate, resting on the meadow. Kun was stretched on the ground further back, with his face held upright. He watched the family from the distance. I observed in his eyes the emotion of nostalgia, as if he were a human being, I could see right in his eyes the desire to go back to his former life. But those days were over. Back or not, now he had changed.

The differences between Kun and him were more obvious. Jumbe had a strong mane around his face and it swayed in the breeze. Kun was an already weaker animal. His body seemed frail and his hair, some of it faded, lacked luster. He could had never beaten Jumbe in a fight."

"Yes, but Jumbe left because he had to learn to be a leader, right?" I asked.

"Not exactly. One neither learns to be a leader nor is born leader. One becomes a leader when one decides to be one. There are those who have decided from the beginning and others who decide at any given time. As much as you know, you are not a leader until you decide. The leader needs to have enough character to take that decision. Our lion had not yet made that decision or had not had the need.

At dusk, Jumbe up quickly and that warned me that something was happening. Behind his family in the bushes, four fisis appeared; four hyenas. The four wailed and knock each other around. They seemed to be in a bad mood. Immediately, Kun stood up to see. The hyenas continued on their path and approached the place where the lions and the offspring were. Kun gave a warning growl. The fisis moved apart and looked at him aggressively, showing their fangs. For a moment, I thought they would really attack, but they chose to move a few feet away, under another tree. However, it was clear that they were not afraid.

The next morning a group of gazelles running through the area to get to the river attracted the attention of the predators. The hyenas became alert rapidly. Kun, who was more attentive to them than what was going on around him, stood up suddenly. The hyenas moved back and forth nervously, eager to attack the

82

gazelles and catch a kill that would serve as lunch. However, although able to hunt in packs by using hunting strategies, they often would choose not to do it, and rather follow the top predators to take advantage and take advantage of the spoils they were leaving.

And Kun stood between hyenas and gazelles. No doubt he wanted the lionesses to ensure food for his family before and the hyenas to try to satisfy their hunger later.

The lionesses crept up to the graceful gazelles followed by the eyes of the hyenas, those of the rest of the family, Jumbe's and mine. The wind seemed to stop to facilitate the task, although the lionesses had initiated the attack cautiously against the wind to prevent their scent to be smelled by the prey. Crouching, their bodies barely raised an inch off the ground, so it was very difficult to see them through the dry grass.

The attack was so accurate and fast than when the gazelles began to flee one of them had already fallen swiped by a claw. At that time Kun allowed the fisis to leave and they went at high speed after gazelles fleeing in retreat. They were skilled hunters. They ran and ran, but the gazelles had already gained a lot of distance. Exhausted, they gradually abandoned the chase until the four were scattered in the horizon. After a few minutes they started back and reunited. They were moaning angry on the road indicating their obvious anger at Kun.

The afternoon passed with a certain tension. The lion family enjoyed their kill under the envious eyes of the hyenas, which were swirling nervously around. Kun had to threaten to attack them several times so that they would not get too close. When the family was satisfied, they withdrew, leaving the remains to the angry hyenas, who threw themselves so hard on the carcass that they seemed to be struggling with a live animal. They competed among themselves for each piece and still clinging to a fine feast, they would focus on the portion their companion was eating and tried to snatch it off. Nothing seemed to please them. The fighting was brutal. The remains were too few and their hunger too great, so they did not seem to be happy. When they finally gave up searching for food in those remains, they went to the lion family in a hostile manner. They were not able to attack, but surrounded them and issued threats. Hyenas do not dare attack lions, but they know to harass others in the distance, bother, request, demand... They have confidence in themselves and in the strength of the group, and therefore sometimes frighten other animals into getting what they want. Kun tried to scare them, but their protests were constant. When he went to one of them, the other three went another way. The lionesses looked at Kun restless, demanding his help, but he could not keep up.

Fortunately, the hyenas decided to withdraw to see if it was not a waste of time. A few yards under the umbrella formed by the thorny acacia branches, they met and continued roaring toward Kun.

Jumbe, who had remained on guard at all times, ready to run to help the family if necessary, decided to move closer quietly during the night.

At dawn, Jumbe was already a few yards from them, and I, just a few feet away from him. The hyenas were even more nervous. Surely, their empty stomachs demanded attention. The lion family had barely slept due to the roar and the constant fighting between the hyenas.

Suddenly, everyone stopped roaring. In the distance, there were two zebras, known around here as punda milia, running on the plain. The hyenas became alert immediately, ready to attack. Kun again stood between them and the prey and threatened them. Nervously, the four gave him furious glances. One of them careened gradually out of sight and launched on him, causing a wound on his back. Still, it shook it off with a blow that left it on the floor. Then he jumped on it and, when it seemed he was going to kill the hyena with a single bite, Jumbe emerged from the bushes. The hyenas, Kun, and family were surprised by the intruder, who ran to the zebras, who fled. Everyone stopped their activities and stood watching.

It was a great show to watch him. His body arched into the air beating the ground with his enormous claws. His golden hair danced around with the speed. Jumbe reached the first zebra and knocked it down, but continued running to the second one, which galloped terrified after seeing its partner fall to ground. When the big cat was on its right, the zebra swerved letting Jumbe run by. He turned back. Now it seemed that he was returning to us. The other punda milia, that was badly wounded, began to get back up after the fall saw them coming towards and also began a limping flight.

The hyenas and the lions understood that Jumbe was leading them to the zebras and went to meet him. It was an easy hunt, the fisis grabbed one and the lions another.

Quickly, two groups of diners were formed, each with the corresponding portion. On one side, there were the lions, their offspring and their young. On the other side, there were the hyenas, which quenched their accumulated appetite.

Kun attacked the hyenas trying to keep them away from the second zebra. Jumbe ran over there and stood between them and the head of the family. Kun looked at him aggressive and suspicious, but did not dare face him. He knew there was nothing for him to do. The happy family surrounded him to show him their love and opened a spot for him to feed. However, Jumbe chose the other kill.

The hyenas, terrified, kept away while Jumbe ate, but their hunger was such that they were approaching step by step.

When one was close enough it tore a small piece of flesh, with fear. Jumbe made no gesture of rejection. Then the rest took to eat.

From my little hideaway, I enjoyed this strange situation. The lion family devoured a kill, while Jumbe shared the other prey with the hyenas."

"But, did Jumbe remain with the hyenas, even after the strong desire he had to see his family?" I asked impatiently.

"No, of course not." He said. When the hyenas were satisfied they joined again and the arguments disappeared. Jumbe then returned with his family, who received him with all sorts of pampering. Kun went into the background. Since that day, Jumbe would leads the family and Kun was to be just another one.

"This was a fantastic story." I congratulated him.

"The, you would be able to tell me five characteristics of Jumbe´s actions?" He asked.

"Yes, I think so." I said, clutching my notebook with the joy of a child who expects to be asked the question he knows the answer to. First, Jumbe showed the example instead of demanding action, because rather than requiring a certain behavior he became the example and showed the hyenas how to achieve results.

"Very good. Nobody is a leader by simply occupying the position of power. This only works with rookies or apprentices, the snakes, for example. The contributors who know how to do their jobs must be shown their own capabilities. And I say show them, because is not always about doing it, but to make sure they seem capable." Said Mwalimu enthusiastically.

"On the other hand, he reconciled his own gain with those of the team. It is important that collaborators understand that their individual gain comes from the gain obtained by the team, and above all, that of the leader. A leader cannot earn his gain in a different manner than the team." I said.

"Perfect. The leader and the team are one and the same, thus its success must come from the same place." He confirmed.

"Besides, the leader is the one who makes them win. With him they get results. As much as we want, teams need to get results. Otherwise, the team is destroyed or finds a more effective leader." I said, convinced.

"Certainly." He said.

"And, of course, Jumbe shares success. He is one of them when it comes to working, but also when enjoying success. He does not stay away, does not fancy himself, does not enjoy it for himself, but he shares it with the whole team. This is what unites them." I said, motivated.

"Yes, it is true. Precisely, you can tell me what characterizes the hyenas compared to the crocodiles" asked him.

"Yes, that too I've noticed. The crocodiles had great skills, but they were dispersed. They were not a team. The hyenas were." I replied.

"Indeed, but we have a final behavior to complete the six faces of the cube." He continued, and showed me sixth wooden cube with a hyena drawn on one side.

"Well, finally, he takes a risk for them. He commits not only to the work or to the target, but to them. Jumbe defends even his own family, risking closing the door on his return." I said, since I understood the responsibility that comes at times with leading a team.

"Exactly, commitment cannot be achieved without committing for the gain of each team member." He said, while handing me the wooden cube piece with a picture of a hyena on one side; another one for the collection.

"You know, this thing about commitment is becoming something special in organizations and teams. Today it seems that everyone is in it for himself only. I think this confirms an idea I had last summer. I was invited then to attend a sail boat race, a very important boat competition, to be held in my country. There were two boats that fought against all odds to reach the finish line first, and I could see the sailors striving and working among them. Beside me there was an announcer that was broadcasting via television and, at one point, he said that the boat in the back was struggling to achieve the commitment. I was stunned, since I did not quite understand what he was trying to say. Another spectator, who was a boat captain, explained to me that the commitment was to reach the boat in front. So the commitment was to get a draw. We often ask employees to commit, but the question is whether the company also commits with them. I've thought about it, since a draw it on my language, in addition to meaning that two things are equal, is also used when two things come together as an act of empathy. Empathy is being able to understand other people's emotions. I am increasingly confident that commitment is not required, is achieved. To achieve this we must give, understanding others and ensuring that what each person wants is similar to what all want. Otherwise rejection would occur." I explained while Mwalimu was listening intently.

"I think it is a good thought. No doubt, good successful organizations are those in which employees internalize the company´s objectives as their own. And when this is not true, it is often due to lack of communication." he answered.

"Certainly; we are so busy checking results and managing the processes that we forget explaining, motivating, selling employees their own work." I completed.

"Yes, it is true. Well, tomorrow I will come back and we will dig a little further into this. You see, this leadership business is becoming more complicated." He said goodbye.

In my notebook, the summary of the talk was written as follows:

• **The leader shows the example instead of demanding action; he becomes the example and shows how to achieve results.**

• **He reconciles his own gains with the gains of the team.**

• **The leader is the one who makes them win. With him they get results.**

• **He shares success, he is one of them when it comes to working, and also when is time to enjoy success.**

• **He commits not only to working or to the goal, but also with the team members.**

VIII.

The kibokos

When I awoke the next morning, I did not notice anything new in the room until the nurse came through the door with breakfast. Then, when I wanted to get out of bed, I realized that the wheelchair was not there. Instead, two crutches were leaning on the side of a chair to the right of the door. Carefully I put my left foot on the floor and spun my hip until the right leg, in plaster from ankle to mid-thigh, hung in the air. I slowly slid weight forward until this motion made me stand up. I walked around the bed on one leg to stand outside the door. There, resting on the back of the chair, were the crutches, and on the seat there was a folded paper.

I stretched my right arm while my left hand was holding the metal bar, which as a handrail delimited the bottom of my bed, and my fingertips I slid the crutch toward me until I could grab it. After grabbing the first one, I used it to get close to the second one, which nearly hit the ground before I could catch it in mid-flight.

That move that seemed simple, was quite an accomplishment for me. I drew a smile across my face as I put the crutches under my arms. The reward for my efforts had given me back my motivation and willingness to walk through the corridors of the hospital.

Previously, curiosity had led me to collect the paper note that was lying on the seat of the chair. I opened it leaning my elbows on the crutches so that I would not fall. In beautiful handwriting the following words were written:

"YOU WILL NOT GET YOUR WISHES

IF YOU DO NOTHING TO OBTAIN THEM

YOU CANNOT GET THAT WHICH YOU HAVE NOT WANTED IN ADVANCE.

I am waiting with a chair for you on the terrace."

During the twelve minutes it took to cross the hallways that separated me from the balcony, I could not stop laughing about the joke Mwalimu had played on me. Certainly the laziness of the holidays had made me forget that I had to regain mobility and should not settle down. When one gets too comfortable one can stop wishing and then apathy overcomes you. If we want our teams to do something we should first get them to do so.

Mwalimu really enjoyed seeing me arrive at the terrace. He was pleased with my decision, and deep down, that he was not wrong. I was then addicted to the Jumbe's stories so I was not prepared to miss that day´s story. As soon as I sat down, exhausted by the effort, Mwalimu dropped a question gazing the landscape in the horizon, like if it was a trivial question

"What animal kills more people each year?"

I thought for a moment about the lion, since we talked about it constantly, but I thought it might be a trick question. So I replied:

"The great white shark."

"It's a good response; without doubt, one derived from the films that have made it famous. Yes, yes, here in Africa we also have movies and television. But I fear that this is the second animal that attacks more humans. The fact that it lives at sea, and the fame it has earned, ensures that people do not approach it a lot. The animal that kills more humans every year is what we call kiboko, and you call, the river horse or hippopotamus.

"Well, I would have never thought so. In my country this an animal has a soft image. In fact, many dolls are made for children with its shape."

"Indeed, it has a friendly reputation because of being an herbivore, and due to its rounded appearance, but when you get close to one of them with its mouth opened in front of you, I can assure you, you would not be thinking about hugging it. Of course, in the case of the hippo, the attacks are defensive and rather due to their fear of man than to their aggressiveness." He said, gesturing with his mouth.

"Today I will tell you a story of Jumbe with the hippos, or as we call them here, the kibokos.

Jumbe returned with his family and never left it again. The lions were proud and happy to have a new protector more powerful than the previous one. They spent several days enjoying the plain. There they enjoyed the shade during the day and evening, and when the temperature dropped; they would go out to hunt food for the pride. Although lions do not need to eat every day and can survive several days without doing so, they took advantage of the opportunity to feed their growing offspring. It was a great place, but lacked enough water. So Jumbe decided that the pride was to moved to another place to settle. As the nomads they were, they took to the road that cut through the different patches of acacias. After a two-day journey, they reached a beautiful place with plenty of undergrowth just a few hundred yards into the territory of John Bald's reserve. In the center, a small lake, which was fed by a spring, served as a meeting point for the animals in the area.

There were several kibokos among them, peaceful-looking animals, but as I said, they can do a lot of damage. They reach about three yards long and two high. They are enormous. Just as Jumbe, his family and I, who was several yards behind, arrived there, we witnessed a brutal spectacle. Two kibokos fought each other by the lake. With their huge jaws open, the big teeth were visible. From there, it seemed that could devour me in a single bite. At first, both hippos were just staring each other down. Facing each other, they showed their strength by opening their jaws as much as possible. Then, growling loudly at each other. Finally, they fought by ramming their teeth into the other. The sound was similar to a traffic accident mixed with the water splashing around. The two beasts fought fiercely with movements that seemed slow, but had such force that made the ground vibrate despite the fact they were in the water. On the shore, the waves caused by the commotion of the fight came all the way to Jumbe's feet. Jumbe watched them and seemed to hesitate, but when one of them reached the neck of the other one and caused a large wound in the skin from which the blood came out gushing, he could no longer remain indifferent.

Jumbe ran around the lake until reaching an area near them and roared as hard as he could. Both animals stopped on their attacks and they looked puzzled. They were so focused on each other that they had not perceived the presence of lions. The rest of the kibokos remained outside, as the fight did not involve them. Perhaps they were hoping that the contenders were sufficiently injured to then present their own candidacy for the leadership of the group. Each of them was in different areas of the lagoon, inspecting and monitoring the others. Together but separated. Like lilies in a pond, they kept getting fatter every day.

Throughout the day the fighting continued. On the rare occasions when one approached another confrontation occurred. I thought Jumbe had attacked willingly to teach them a lesson, but in the lagoon the kiboko had the upper hand. Still, the fact is that they obeyed him, and every time he roared they would stop their fights.

The next morning Jumbe departed, leaving the family behind. At first I thought he was gone only to explore, but after two hours of waiting I thought, wondering, thinking if he had deserted the family. But five or six hours later, when I was looking for my own food, I heard the deep sound of the heavy and repetitive walking of a tembo. The tembo, also known as ndovus are what you call elephant.

I came back rapidly where the lion family was resting in fear of being attacked. From the brush, past the lake, appeared the huge figure of a tembo, poking his magnificent head. The bushes were literally crushed by its body, which was not perturbed as it rose above the bush, which minutes earlier, was stiff and prickly. When you see so strong a silhouette appear, one that nothing stands in its way, your body is paralyzed. On seeing it, the kibokos drifted slowly and gathered on the opposite bank. It was the first time I saw them together without quarreling among themselves. However, the lions kept calm, as if they did not see it or hear it. Then, after the tembo, I saw why they were so relaxed: Jumbe was following it from a short distance, as if to lead it to them.

I was amazed, I thought that Jumbe had gone for help to teach them a lesson, but this behavior seemed very courageous, and if I could be sure of anything, was his valor. For the moment, and throughout the afternoon and night, he had managed quiet down the kibokos. The hippos had gathered in a small area of the lake and were forced to share the food they had. If before, even though they had more than enough in their area, they fought to get more, and now they had to share about one-tenth among them. If they had not been forced, they would had never done anything like that.

With the new dawn the lake was completely different from two days ago. The constant noise of fighting had disappeared. The Lions enjoyed their games and jokes, the kibokos had learned to share a portion of the lake and the elephants frolicked in the mud. Soon after, Jumbe went back to the tembo and led it behind the trees. They did not take long to reappear. The elephant with its trunk was dragging a tree log, which, based on its appearance, seemed to have been a long time drying on the ground. Seeing this, it seemed that anyone could lift it into the air with one hand, but the reality was very different.

Jumbe gestured, and the tembo deposited the log on the surface of the lake. With noise, the log sank speedily to and resurfaced immediately. The waves reached all the way to the kibokos who looked with amazement and fear. The rustic boat floated slowly toward them. As they approached, they were getting more nervous; and some got ready to stand behind, others, who were more determined separated and remained in the forefront. The tree moved slowly towards them, until it ran into the snout of the first one. Although the log was of a considerable size, its speed was minimal, so I stopped in front of him. For a few seconds, everyone, including the elephant, watched for its reaction. Feeling watched, it turned its head trying to shake off the log and forward the stare towards the others. The large log turned on the water until it rested horizontally in front of several kibokos. Now several of them were standing before the log. On the left, the biggest of them pushed forward, but the log was met with two heads that stopped from spinning. Then the three rammed it. The log sank, rolled over itself, and reappeared in front of them.

The young lions, who watched the scene from the bank, jumped for joy. The hippos seemed clumsy and useless in that situation.

The kibokos tried for several minutes to shake it off, but every time one of them would attempt it, it was returned by another. When they were tired enough, Jumbe ran along the bank to them and went into the water. He certainly was not a good swimmer, but the truth is that it was the only lion I have seen floating. He barely got close to them and placed himself in the middle. Leaning on the kiboko that were at both sides, he pushed the log, which broke away a few inches from them. Immediately, the two kibokos pushed forward at the same time, so again it broke away. They both looked at each other and then looked at their mates. Several of them pushed back again at the same time and this time it separated further. After discovering the method, they changed their attitude and began to move faster. Two of those who were behind joined the group and pushed the log. Two further shoves and they succeeded in bringing the log to the bank, right at the foot of the tembo. The tembo looked at and looked at Jumbe, who had come back to solid ground. He raised his face, satisfied, and slowly walked to the log. The elephant backed up a few yards, as if it had given up. The kibokos enjoyed it while rubbing each other's body. Together they had pushed back the ndovu.

While they were throwing water, were bumping each other and having fun, Jumbe took the opportunity to leave with the elephant, but soon returned with freshly plucked green bushes rolled in the elephant's trunk that it deposited in the shore. Then the tembo left the same way he had come.

That very night the kibokos came out of the lake to graze and devoured scrub with pleasure."

"Well, so they leave the water to eat!" I exclaimed, surprised, imagining those bodies on land.

"Of course, they ensure that the weeds do not invade the lake and the river. Every night they come out to graze and keep the grass in balance. Did you think they ate fish?" He asked, laughing.

"Well, no. The truth is that I never stopped to think what they ate, but calling them river horses, it makes sense they eat grass," I joked.

"Of course the hard part is to riding them." He said with a laugh.

The image of a race between Mwalimu and I, both riding a kiboko made me laugh with him. At that moment the doctor appeared on the terrace, who ordered me to return me to the room as lunch time was approaching and with the crutches it would take me longer than on the wheelchair. I regretted having to leave Mwalimu at this fun time. I got up, leaning on the crutches, under the watchful eye of my companions, and I started to go back to my white cell.

"Wait, you forgot something!" Mwalimu, who seemed to feel as bad about the interruption, called my attention when I was about to go up the aisle. On his hand he held the seventh wooden cube with the face of a kiboko.

"Oh, yes. Thanks." I said as the doctor picked up the strange object to prevent me let go of the crutches.

"Well, but in order to keep it, you must answer the usual question." He said, turning his face in the suspicious manner.

"Of course, the five behaviors I've seen in the story. Well, hum..." I joked, as if it was hard for me to find the answers. Let's see: first he avoids and control conflicts, suspicions and jealousies. A team must be united and Jumbe stops their confrontations" I stated.

"Well, but this was easy." He said.

"The second step is to create a group identity, he gathers the kibokos and shows them a goal or a common enemy. By bringing in the elephant, the hippos no longer see each other as competitors and team up to fight with others." I said.

"Very good. This can be done with a common enemy, but also with a vision, goal or a mission. The important thing is that it is common, of course, and a challenge for everyone." He said firmly.

"Right. Another behavior was to force them to perform a group task. Something they had to do together. That forces them to interact, to help each other. Each one by itself could not move the log, and they have to do it together." I explained.

"Correct, the work of a leader is also to keep the group together. The leader who does not see confrontation between individuals or factions in his organization or, even worse, does nothing to prevent it, ends up losing his leadership and just being hated by all." He replied sternly.

"Certainly." I agreed; having lived it. Another behavior is to change the routine, turning work into fun. The hippos were stuck in the water and bored; they knew how to do the job and accepted Jumbe as a leader, but they were so tired of doing the same thing that now they were facing each other. The job, the task, what we do, is what motivates people the most. A leader must convert that into motivation. I remember that competition bonuses between salespeople to re-motivate them, was an example of how to turn the daily routine into play." I continued.

"Great. Work should be an incentive for people, not a punishment, and that is the job of leader. It is also critical that employees know the importance of their work. Many times the boss addresses them only to correct them and not to flatter them. People like knowing that what they do has value. He must value, in other words give it value, but also show them what it's worth. Show what it means to other departments or to customers whenever possible." He said.

"I think that's a great idea. And after that, the fifth behavior is to perform a joint celebration, even outside the common area. That all celebrate the results as a single person." I ended.

"Perfect, I see that you are a skilled listener. Tomorrow we'll meet again. And I'll tell you how to lead an animal more powerful than oneself."

And alone in my room, I reviewed these five issues:

• **The leader prevents and controls conflict, suspicion and envy.**

• **He creates group identity, establishing a vision, goal or a common mission.**

• **He imposes a group task, for the members to interact and help.**

- He changes the routine to make work fun.

- He makes a joint celebration, even outside the common area.

IX.

The tembos

The truth is that I was tired of that room. After breakfast, I got up and walked to the window with the crutches under the arms. Since then, I had disconnected from my work, but was eager to return home.

I heard that somebody opened the door and I turned around. It was the doctor on duty in the morning.

"Good morning. How are you?" He asked routinely

"Well, you see... Here, dancing." I said wryly.

"Do not worry. I know you are uncomfortable, but today I am bidding you good news." He said noticing my discontent.

"Sorry. I'm just a little tired of being locked in." I recognized.

"It's normal, normal. Sit down, I would like to examine the knee. It has been immobilized for eight days, and sure, you are wishing to leave." He said sarcastically.

After examining the leg and moving it, he asked a nurse to bring an instrumentation cart. It took him a couple of minutes to cut through the cast and removed it like it was a skirt. After that, he washed the leg with a sponge dipped in water and disinfectant. The knee looked more packed due to the compression of the cast and still had showed the sutures from the surgery. The doctor said I had healed very well and the next day he would take away the sutures.

"You still have to keep the knee still, so I'll bring you a special brace. I am not going to put another cast because you could not go on a plane with it and I guess you really want to get back home. As far as I know, tomorrow afternoon, if all goes well, when we remove the sutures, I can release you. However, you have to have keep the knee still for another ten days and then you should do rehabilitation therapy." He said kindly, while taking notes.

"Thank you, doctor." I said truly happy.

"Elephant." He said without taking his eyes from the report he was writing.

" Elephant?" I asked, puzzled.

"An elephant, you're missing an elephant." He repeated, pointing his pen to the cubes I had on my nightstand.

"Oh, yeah, thanks." I replied.

Snakes, leopards, monkeys, wildebeest, crocodiles, hyenas and hippos in the form of cubes lined up on the table forming a strange wooden train. Certainly, an elephant was missing; an elephant and, of course, a lion.

As Mwalimu had not arrived, I decided to leave to the hallway and walk to the terrace. I liked watching the landscape, especially to get out of that room. Upon arrival, I found that Mwalimu was waiting for me with a wooden cube at the center of the same old table. I could not help but smiling when I saw that one side displayed the silhouette of an elephant.

108

"Good morning." He greeted me politely.

"Good morning." I said, and sat by his side.

"I see that your leg is much better. I am glad to know that soon will go home." He said when he noticed the new bandage over my battered limb.

"Yes. In fact, the doctor told me that tomorrow I may be discharged. The truth is that on the one hand, I'm glad, because I have to be back at home, but on the other hand, I will miss your great stories. I'm very intrigued to know more about Jumbe." I said sincerely.

"Well, the normal thing to do is to return home. I will be glad that you do it because I know that over there, you will be better off. Also, today I am going to tell the last story about Jumbe and tomorrow I will come back again in the morning to chat with you. If you'd prefer, I will prepare everything for Mbuto to come by the hotel to pick up your things and talk to the travel agency to schedule your flight."

"Thank you, I would be very nice if Mbuto would stop by the hotel because then I would not have to go. As it started out, the trip was to take twelve days and the return flight was scheduled for just after tomorrow, so if all goes well, I could even use the one already scheduled, and they would not have to deal with new travel schedules." I said gratefully.

"Well, then I will proceed to tell you what happened after Jumbe left the kiboko lagoon.

Jumbe had used a tembo to achieve his aims with the kibokos. But this tembo was not just any elephant, it was the candidate to lead his herd. Jumbe had met it earlier in during his lone journey. The herd was in constant danger from poachers who depleted many herds in search of ivory. Jumbe knew that survival of the herd depended directly on the skills of the leader, a tembo smart enough to avoid the lurking dangers.

The tembo left when he learned that he had fulfilled his role in the lagoon, but Jumbe knew it owed a debt of gratitude to him. So, a day later, when he found that the kibokos were collaborating with each other and had fun playing with the log in the water, he left looking for it accompanied by his family, and I tagged along.

I realized that true leaders always hang around with top performers and are not afraid to surround themselves with the most powerful, but quite the contrary, they search that.

After a few hours, in the distance, we spotted the herd of elephants. In total there were three females, two males and an offspring. Each male attempted to guide the herd in a different direction. One of them wanted to take a seemingly easy way, probably created by the SUVs, while the other one, which we already knew, opted for another seemingly worse path. The

110

females looked at them without being able to decide which one to follow. Little by little we got closer until we were in sight. Immediately the elephant recognized Jumbe.

I suppose you know about the tembo's great capacity to remember things, even recalling any animal fifty years after seeing it, right?

Well, Jumbe ran to the second elephant and stood before him. Then he stood on his hind legs and growled showing his teeth while throwing fierce clawing in the air in a threatening manner. The elephant suddenly understood that this road was not easy to use, but did not give up right away, pointed his snout in the air and let out a puff of air that resonated across the entire valley. However, Jumbe roared again showing his determination. The elephant looked around for an exit, but the females were frightened by the lion and had moved closer to another male elephant. It had no choice but to face the lion or join the rest of the herd. For a moment, the elephants looked at each other, it seemed they were talking.

The fact is that elephants have a communication system through subsonic waves that man cannot hear. A researcher taught me that; she had come here once and made a recording. When amplified, the sound is heard as a deep sound, like a bass.

Well, finally the elephant left the rest, but they did not choose the second path. When they went to take the road following the first tembo, Jumbe again ran into the road and blocked it. However, this time the elephant decided to continue walking between the two paths.

Really, being a leader means that choosing the paved way is not always the right thing to do, for then others will try to get passed you. The true leader is one who is able to take different paths, even if difficult, or build new roads. That is the one people want to follow and hesitate to overcome. There are no shortcuts to being a leader.

The elephant was covered by the brush until it reached a clearing and continued by it crossing it. Throughout the path, Jumbe and his family followed the herd from a distance, but in view of the elephant, who occasionally looked at them to ensure it was still there. As they walked through the clear, the baby elephant, with its trunk, grabbed the tail of the female elephant in front, and she, in turn, the one of the second male elephant. They formed a very compact herd that crossed the plain.

Elephants are large nomads able to walk hundreds of miles to get to a place that they like. On that occasion they were going to a place where they had never been, for the entire canyon did not show signs of a previous herd. Those animals of over eight thousand pounds in weight left tracks everywhere they had trodden. They walked many miles until it got dark and then stopped to rest, which I was thankful for, since I had never walked so much.

112

At dawn, they resumed to the road. Not many minutes went by until the tembos herd met an artificial barrier. It was a five-feet-high metal fence that ran along the access path between the hills enclosing the valley. The fence was not high, and of course, strong enough to prevent an ndovu from knocking it down, but it looked new and they did not know what to do."

"Even elephants fear change." I said.

"That's right. Upon seeing the situation, Jumbe came up to them. Just a few hundred yards to the right, just where vehicle tracks had blazed a path through the grass, there was a nine-foot opening in the fence. Jumbe went there and verified it was accessible. Slowly, he went through the opening and ran down the other side until returning to the same height. The elephants saw him through the metal fence, but instead of rejoicing, they became more nervous. I guess they thought they were alone, that he could achieve it, but they could not, even though they had not tried.

Jumbe did not give up and returned with them. By means of threats and roars he led the herd to the door as if he was a shepherd and they were the sheep. When they got there, he forced the tembo which had led the way, through the opening in the fence. Despite his indecision, it ended up crossing over to the other side. Its first feeling was one of uncertainty, but then, after it turned around several times as if it wanted to check that the other side was as strong as the side it came from. The rest of the

113

herd looked at it expectantly, quietly. Jumbe walked a few yards away. The tembo turned tracked back its steps and met with five other elephants, rubbing against them; then, went through the opening again, without being out of sight. The youngest took the initiative and went after him. The rest of them followed right after with caution."

"I understand, you are trying to say that the herd would have never crossed together, but if you let the leader cross over, the rest will follow, right?" I asked.

"Of course. It is true."

"When all they all took to the path and headed away, I also crossed the fence as well. It was an area I already knew and I had been there many times. Just next to the opening, to the right, in the pole that held the metal mesh, there was a wooden sign that read: 'John Bald's Animal Reserve.'

I continued walking in the hills along the trail. The end of the road leads to another valley dominated by a river that crosses it from side to side, and provides water to hundreds of animals that live there. It is a great place where animals can live in peace and never lack water, as some springs keep feeding the stream bed. When I arrived, the elephants had gone to a small pond that watered the creek near a set of trees, while Jumbe, the lionesses and the rest of the group stayed away. At that time, I noticed that one of the lionesses went running into the trees. The tembo immediately changed their slow pace and launched onto something. From a distance, I could see what was happening, but far away, behind the trees, I saw my son's, Mbuto, jeep and ran. The rest, you already know."

"So you were there." I said, surprised.

"Yes, but I could do nothing but help my son to bring you here."

"What I still don't understand is why he attacked us." I asked.

"Well. I think it was not due to anything specific. Young leaders, those who are not yet ready, are lack self-confidence and are dangerous, they fear losing their position and attack occasionally to defend it. That's why they are not real leaders. Fortunately, Jumbe was there watching for any reaction." He said.

"Yes. The truth is I don't know how I would have been able to stop the elephant's onslaught." I said, recalling the scene.

"That is very difficult. It's like stopping a derailed runaway train. The only person who can do it is the engineer who runs it from the beginning. But tell me, what behaviors have you seen in today's story?"

"The truth is that this time I've seen many." I pointed, with notebook in my hands.

"First, Jumbe promoted the leader of the herd. He finds and chooses the ideal candidate and promotes it internally in the team. When the herd is at fork in the road, the lion requires the group to follow his chosen one. In fact, it does so in making it take a new path. The real success of a leader is to find a worthy and prepared replacement in time. I have seen many organizations that are slowly deteriorating because leaders are unable to transfer their leadership. That even goes against themselves, because it prevents them to continue growing. There is no better way to grow than to be pushed from below by your own staff; as Kun did with Jumbe. Bad bosses are determined to trample and to prevent the rise of its employees and that makes them stagnate. If, however, they are able to advance them, they themselves are benefiting.

Secondly, after forcing it to build its own road, he continues providing safety for its group, although remaining at a distance. Sometimes, the new leader needs to have a backup in order to develop as such. In this case, Jumbe acted as a backup to the group.

However, there is a third feature: He showed what needed to be done, but they did let themselves. Leaders set the expected results, but let the new leader establish its own mechanisms.

Fourth, he monitored the behavior consistently and assisted when necessary. For example, when the herd ran into the

116

fence, he ran to help them and teach them to overcome it. Thus, the leader appears only when needed and leaves the group and its new leader to handle the rest.

Finally, he let it made a mistake, but corrected it immediately and without hesitation. When the elephants attacked us, your son and I, Jumbe ran to save us, but at the same time he was saving the leader of the pack. He was correcting them and letting them know that this was not necessary."

"Very good. I appreciate the fact that not only you have understood it, but also your words contain no bitterness."

"The truth is I cannot get angry because we had invaded their privacy. He probably was as scared as us." I said.

"I am really glad about that and that you feel better. Tomorrow we'll meet again and so you can show me the wood piece collection. I hope you'll like them as a memento of your stay here?" He added, handing me the eighth wooden cube.

"Oh, yes. Believe me they will serve to remind me of this country and, above all, you and Jumbe." I said.

"Oh, another thing, this evening you should think about what is the proper order to place each of those pieces. I already gave some hints a few days ago." He said mockingly, recalling it.

In my notebook I wrote the summary as follows:

• The leader must be able to train and promote new leaders.

• He has to offer them safety from a distance.

• He sets the expected results, but lets the new leader establish its own mechanisms.

• He controls and assists when necessary.

• He lets them make mistakes, and corrects them.

X.

The scheme

I woke up happier than usual. That day was the last in the hospital and although I had been treated well, I wanted to leave it. Africa had left me forever marked, not only by the scar on my knee, but also by the friendliness of its people.

After a cleaning myself up and eating breakfast, Mwalimu and his son Mbuto arrived.

"Good morning." Said Mbuto, his face filled with happiness. Glad to see me really recovered.

"Hello." I replied, grateful for his return.

"We've brought your luggage." He said, and left it in a corner near the window. I could not remember how many things I had brought and upon seeing at that moment the huge size of the suitcase that contained them, I felt ridiculous.

"How are you?" Mwalimu asked with interest.

"Well, I woke up with a lot of energy. Today is a strange day. On the one hand, I am very happy because it is almost time for my return, but on the other hand, I admit that I will miss you." "The accident has been hard, but it's been a pleasure talking with you." He explained.

"I understand. We both know that life is like the sea that is constantly bringing waves, some are good, and some are bad." He answered, trying to be condescending.

"Yes, and I think it is best not to think about the waves, but about the destination you want to reach. Looking at the horizon and swimming or navigating without stopping upon each wave. If you see a project clearly, the waves, incidents, are more than just elements in the landscape." I said, following his metaphor to match his deep talks. He smiled back with gratitude.

"I see you have the wooden pieces on the table." He said, approaching them to change the subject.

"Yes. I have been placing them in order, one after another, as you told me the stories. This way, I went over it mentally in the evening. I think they all have a common link. You were trying to tell me that not all teams are equal and that each one requires a particular form of leadership, right?" I said, being a smartass. In a way, I wanted to show him my interest and appreciation.

"Well, actually I see that you've been thinking about it. In fact they are ingredients, how to mix them is all have to know. Like a cake, the whole is better than each of its parts. All pieces are part of a whole that is greater than the sum of them. It's like parts in a car. Each is valuable, but if not properly attached, set in place and working properly, the car will never start. Do you understand?" He interrogated me, making me think like he normally did.

I think so. In fact, I'd like to tell you a story. "When I was a child, I had an uncle whom I admired, uncle Peter. I remember every year he would appear at home showing off the new car he had bought. The whole family would go down to the street to see it and we got inside until we could fit no more people inside the car. Then he used to let me get behind the wheel and I saw that as something very difficult. I could barely move it, because the power steering did not exist.

So when I sat there poking my bangs around the dashboard, he would tell us driving stories. "I've driven at 100 miles per hour;" "I almost ran off the road on a curve"...

One year, when I was older, the day before my uncle arrived, I told my father that I really wanted to see my uncle because I wanted to teach me to drive. My father said he could do it himself and I answered that I preferred Peter to do it because he was a great driver.

That should have offended my father for he took my hand and walked me out to see our car. It wasn't a new car as my uncle's, it was a few years old, but it was in showroom condition. He sat at the wheel and told me:

"This car has spent six years with us and has traveled 1200,000 miles. Can you see the gauges? They showed the speed, rpms and, most importantly, the engine temperature. I will tell you later everything you need to know about them. Below, you have the pedals: clutch, brake and accelerator. You see, son, every part of a car has a purpose and you must understand them and use them for the car to work well."

"Yeah right, but this car does not go very fast." I replied.

"Son, a good driver is not the one who goes faster, but the one who goes farther. Going fast is easy, especially when you have a new car. The hard part is that the car is finely tuned and runs year after year." He said.

Today, every time I drive to the office I remember those words and think about the number of managers who run their companies like my uncle's driving. Concerned to achieve maximum results, they destroy team after team. Of course, each year they boast their numbers. But management must be measured in time, not just in one fiscal period. It's easy to change teams to succeed. The tricky thing is to keep it and develop it. Make it so that each year they achieve better results.

Indeed, my uncle was a fast driver, but every two years he had to change cars because one part or another would fail and repairing it would involve a very large cost.

All managers must consider, in addition to their results, rotation in their teams because sooner or later the costs will be higher than the results. My uncle had it easy, he could go from dealership to dealership and buy another, but right now, in this type of labor market, it is very difficult to find people to replace team members." I said, pleased to have narrated a story.

"It's a good story that teaches many things. As you yourself said, we must understand each part. Let's talk about them, the first one, and the one about the snakes or nyoka. This part, which represents a type of team, a group of people working in an organization, what characteristics do they have?" He asked, and took in his hand the piece drawn with a snake, while his son sat down in another chair and looked at his father with admiration.

"It's easy. Snakes are not even a team. Each goes its own way, acts on impulse, each does whatever it wants and they confront Jumbe, the leader." I said quickly.

"Very good. Indeed, snakes did not have skills; they consumed more than what they really needed, and did not coordinate amongst them and that harmed all of them, and also they attacked Jumbe. As you say, more than a team, they would be individuals acting alone and without much knowledge. And what about the leopards or chui? He asked again, leaving the previous piece and picking up the second one, the leopard, to show it to me.

"Well, the two are like brothers, but they are not very skilled, you could say they were learning, and they did accept Jumbe." I explained, with doubts.

"You're not misguided. Leopards are fantastic animals, capable of running at high speed. However, they are not as strong as lions or hyenas. In fact, sometimes, the hyenas are able to steal their prey. In the story, they were not so adept at toppling the rhino and Jumbe himself shows them how. Do you remember what differentiates them from the snakes?" He asked, with the leopard wooden piece in his right hand.

"Well, the snakes do not know what to do, and they do not accept the lion, so the only difference is that they do not get along with each other and the leopards are very close. In fact, they hunt together." I said.

"Exactly, the difference between a piece of wood and the other is what we call kabila, solidarity among team members. This is one of the main characteristics of teams. Good teams, those that get the best results, show great solidarity among them. They feel part of a common goal, have habits or rules of behavior that everyone accepts and, ultimately, form a separate unit that can be represented by distinctive characteristics." He said.

"I see. Does it mean that one of the characteristics that I should pursue is that the team is united and adds to more than the sum of its components? And that it has his own character?" I asked, actually confirming it.

"Yes, it's not just something that you must promote, but that you must manage to distinguish one type of team from another." He said. Let's look at the following piece." He put the leopard piece to the right of the snake and took the one for monkey.

"Well, the monkeys do accept Jumbe and fear him, but do not know what to do and are a bit lost. Moreover, they were not getting along among them. So they are different than the snakes because they are not supportive, and distinct from other leopards because they accept the leader." At that moment, I began to understand that the pieces actually had an order.

"Yes, it is true. As you say, they have no solidarity because they are not united. Therefore, they cannot be next to the leopards. This time, the difference is the acceptance or what we call around here pokea." He said, and put the monkey piece right in front of the snake thus covering it. Now the table had the monkey piece behind the snake piece, and to the right of that, the leopard's piece.

"I understand. So snakes are the starting point because they have no solidarity or accept the leader. To the right, the leopards, which do have sympathy, but that did not accept the leader. But in front of them would be the monkeys, who have no sympathy, but do accept Jumbe. That means that there are two axes to place the teams: one, the ones characterized by solidarity that go from left to right, and on the other, acceptance, running from back to front." I said, expressing my thoughts out loud while my engineer brain made a three-dimensional drawing in the air.

"Exactly." He said with a smile.

"Sure." I continued. Then the part of the buffalo is placed in the hole in front, just ahead of the leopard, because among them there is a high solidarity, they go together, move together and accept the orders of the leader, but cannot do things right." I said, cheerful.

"Indeed. They are settled and have little initiative, but they obey the leader. This team is very common in consolidated organizations that often have many rules to address the lack of initiative with procedures." He said.

"I know what you're talking about. This type of team requires someone to motivate them and make them move, because today change is constant and they move too slowly. In addition, there is a law of nature that says if you cannot keep pace your environment you will probably disappear." I admitted.

"Right. But, in order to understand all the teams that can arise in an organization, you must form a cube formed by these parts. That's why I said that they all form a larger piece. You already have one part, but that's only half. Now we need to build the upstairs. Remember how the crocodile team was." He said, taking the piece with a crocodile drawn on it.

"Sure, of course, crocodiles know what to do, they do are skilled hunters and swimmers. One is notable for its strength, another one for its skill with the tail, yet another one for its speed, and the last one by the way it can swim up to catch a fish. However, between them they do not cooperate and do not accept Jumbe, who has to teach them what they gain so they get the team's goal, which is to remove the log." I said, pleased, as Mwalimu placed the piece on with the snake drawing.

"Very good. That's the difference. In this case they have no solidarity or kabila, or accept the leader, or pokea, but they have great skills, erevu, and therefore, confidence in themselves. Erevu is ability and knowledge. Sometimes a team does not have sufficient skill or knowledge, although it believes it has it, that is, its members have much confidence in themselves. Then their behavior is similar." He said, lifting the piece with a hyena off the table.

"I understand; that is, there is a third axe to distinguish the teams that go from the bottom up and that would be skill or confidence in themselves. Thus, teams that do not have it would be on the floor below the cube, while those who trust in themselves, or those who do know what to do, or know the technique or have the experience, would be up." I said, already thinking about specific people in my organization.

"Yes, it is true. Solidarity, following the leader's orders, and ability. Those are the three characteristics that differentiate teams. Based on them we can extract eight different teams. What is next?" He asked, giving me the responsibility to ensure his theory was understood.

"The part with the hyena has to go on top of the leopard because they also know how to run and chase zebras, so they have skills; they get along well and are supportive, but do not accept Kun, the other lion, which supposedly led them at the time. Therefore, to are to the right of the crocodiles." I said.

"Exactly, you have actually understood the stories." He said after placing the piece and picking up another one with a hippo.

"The hippos or kiboko also have great skills and strength, but are disjointed and even confront each other. They spend the day complaining and protesting. Yes, they fear and obey Jumbe. Thus, they have skills, acceptance, but lack solidarity. Therefore, they are placed in front of the crocodiles, just above the monkeys." I said firmly, getting ahead of his question.

"Well, well. Actually this is a very specific type of team and, like the buffalo, too common. These are individuals who know what to do and very well, but are stuck in the lake. Too much time too much skill and causes envy and confrontation." He added.

"Yeah, I admit it. The same occurs with people with seniority and hope to reach a position of power over others. When they do not reach it, they become dangerous, because they are pessimistic, suspicious, only see the negative, forget the good things and complain about everything; they criticize, even in secret among them." I continued, think aloud again about specific individuals I had known in my career.

"True, and are they terrible with new people; they discourage by telling them only the bad things that have happened." He explained while grabbing the last piece and showing it to me.

"Finally, the tembo, the big elephant. It can only be placed in a hole; the one meant for it for having skill, solidarity and acceptance. Truly, it knows what to do, is in solidarity with the herd, since it never abandons them, goes back to them, and accepts Jumbe's orders." I assured as Mwalimu placed the piece in the last hole, forming a cube, two wooden pieces high by two wide and two deep, the leadership cube.

"Great. You are really clever." Said Mbuto, excited.

"Yes. You have grasped quickly the characteristics of the team. As you said, each requires different leadership. Therefore, it is necessary to exercise cubic leadership. That is, the leader must base his behavior according to each team and he must take into account the three pillars: solidarity, acceptance and skill. Each team requires a specific behavior, and therefore, different leadership: the nyoka teams, the snakes need to be addressed firmly and required rigid leadership.

"I understand. The leader must be very strict. Establish what to do. Monitor and act promptly on any deviation." I confirmed. Of course, I had seen this behavior in many bosses, so I could describe it well.

"Exactly. But remember that in this leadership, it is very important to be fair and treat everyone equally. Otherwise it is likely to cause suspicion and lose leadership." He answered.

"Of course, and that leadership must not be permanent, right?" I asked.

"Indeed. Leadership is to be used for rapid progress of the team; to develop it into a new style of leadership. For example, if they become consolidated as a team and acquire greater solidarity, they will become a chui team, leopards. This can happen because they know each better, because they discover a common end in their functions, or simply because they join the leader. When they reach that type of team, you need to strengthen the position of the leader. Show your worth, but not from the standpoint of the organization. You must act with emotional intelligence and empathy. If you want to win the team over, you must show they gain a personal benefit for having you as a leader. In this case, they need to be protected, and you need to lead them as a protector." He pointed to my amazement.

"Sure, but if they do not have solidarity but accept the orders of the leader, they will be a single team and perform other behaviors." I said, following his theory. I never asked myself that the leader should provide personal value to the team and not just the result."

"I see you understand. The tumbuli teams, the monkeys needed to be told exactly what to do, since they mimic the leader and he must be their role model. But beware, because everyone wants to learn, but hates being taught." He said, giving me the floor again.

"Exactly. You have to be a role model and then have them role-play under your supervision. In this way they will be confident in what they do." I continued.

"Very good. You see, in each team, the leader works on their growth, improves it. The leader is a guide and therefore must lead the team somewhere. Otherwise he would only be another manager or coordinator. The true leader is the one leading the team to a better place." He said.

"I see what you mean. The fourth team would have high solidarity and high acceptance, and therefore the leader must develop their skill or confidence levels." I suggested for him to continue.

"The kongoni teams, the buffalo, needed innovation, someone to guide them and be their guide. They tend to be conformist and often bogged down in procedures and paradigms. It's time to break that way of seeing reality and show them a different one that attracts them.. Remember that a team is obedient. This is where the true leader shows his value to the organization." He answered.

"Yes, indeed. There are many managers that select teams of this type. Because they are obedient and do what the manager says, he can also become a buffalo and get stuck in one behavior. However, in times of constant change, it would be like if someone stays in a branch off the bank of a river that is growing, sooner or later he will drown." I said.

"Good comparison. In these cases, one can swim against the current, which will be very difficult to break, and swim to shore or take advantage of it to reach the edge faster or to go further." He pointed.

"Let's talk about the teams that do have skill or confidence. The crocodile team would be the first team, they have skill, but lack solidarity and do not accept the leader." I explained.

"The mamba teams, the crocodiles are very clever, but lack support, and they can only be convinced by using their skills and involving them for them to see that they are better off with the help of other member's skills. It is very important to show them a common goal that interests them all. Make them achieve by joining their skills, and celebrating jointly." He explained.

"I understand. That would make them come together as a team." I said.

"But remember that here, we are trying to develop solidarity, but also acceptance, since the leader must engage with them and, if possible, excel." He clarified.

"Of course, another team would be the hyenas. I understand this clearly, since I see my direct team reflected here. They have so many skills that now they ask me about everything." I said, almost asking for help.

"Indeed, the fisi teams, the hyenas, require a leader to demonstrate their skills, forcing them to use theirs, and they acting as an example for improvement, and considering him at the same time as part of the group. What they need is to regain their acceptance by the leader, and that can only be achieved by demonstrating and committing to them. They feel that the leader is part of the group and not an outsider who is above them." He answered accurately.

"I see. At the other end would be the hippo team, which accepts the leader and has skill, but not solidarity. Here, group therapy is required." I suggested.

"The kiboko teams, the hippos are stagnant teams and need a leader that holds them together, one that unites them and motivates them with new challenges and celebrations. They tend to master their work, and just need mental challenges to make them stay active. Otherwise, they will be using their energy in defending or attacking each other." He explained.

"Then the leader has to be the one providing new challenges. That is really difficult. It is very hard to be constantly looking for new ideas." I confessed.

"Well, that is the job of a leader, but he must also try to delegate it to the team. You can always improve something; you must encourage them to have the initiative. But remember that the main task is to unite them. It is very important that they are a community, identifying themselves as a unified group, even different from the others, to contribute something to others and have a common-sense and purpose." He explained.

"Of course." I nodded, still thoughtful. "And lastly, the elephant piece, the team of the delegation. Am I wrong?" I asked.

"It's not that simple. The tembo teams, the elephant, are the prepared teams that are afraid to make decisions, and therefore, require a patron leader to support them and push them. They are the engines of change, but we that must demanded of them. As ever, the work of the leader is to make them overcome barriers, forcing them to create new paths and trying to facilitate it for them." He said.

"Yes, but it's like allowing them no longer being my team," I complained.

"It's much more than that. You must encourage them even if they finish above their own leader. But remember that the leader must make them perform on their own, and mostly watch that they are on track. That is the greatest risk, as his power and insecurity causes them sometimes to act impulsively. Remember that Jumbe saved your life." He explained, leaving me stunned. After so many years thinking about it, I could not imagine that leadership could be represented so clearly.

"I understand. Then the cube has three dimensions: solidarity, acceptance and ability or confidence. The width of the cube corresponds to the solidarity of the team members; the more solidarity, the more to the right. The depth corresponds to the acceptance of orders from the leader; the greater the acceptance, the more to the front of the cube. Finally, the height corresponds to the skill and confidence of each team member; the more confident, the greater the height." And in saying this, I took a notebook from the bedside table's drawer and drew three lines on a sheet still staring dumbfounded at the wooden pieces that were arranged on top of each other on the table.

"Exactly. This is how Jumbe will lead, the cubic leader." Mwalimu said, smiling. But there is a fourth axis. An axe that goes diagonally from the start of the cube, past the place where the three axes intersect and reaches the opposite end, just at the apex of the tembo piece. It is the axis of independence, which moves you away from the origin. The more skills you have, the greater the leader acceptance, the greater the solidarity, and the more possibilities to act alone." He explained before my drawing.

"And the work of a leader is to move from a cube to another. But, is there an ideal road? What is the first cube and which follows?" I asked.

"No, there really is not one way. Each team can develop into one or other piece. There are many factors that cannot be controlled, from the personality of the members up to the

136

external situation in which they are. So you have to constantly analyze in which piece you are, and act accordingly." He clarified.

"Now, I see. Then leading teams is not that complicated. I only have to know what type of team it is and follow the appropriate guidelines." I said gratefully.

"Well, is not so simple. True leadership is knowing how to decide on what to do. Leadership is a choice and not an image. It has little to do with charisma. Leadership is not a question of knowledge, but of decision and character. Character is like a language. We are all born with one and we educate ourselves with it, but we can learn others and use them when we need them." He said.

"Of course. It is never the fiercest lion who leads the group, but the smartest, which is capable of achieving the objectives. Leadership is getting people to do things more efficiently. To do this, we must first make them believe they are even able to make things better. Everyone we can do improve performance, we just need a leader; someone who motivates and excites us." Said Mbuto, and pointed to his father.

"I've always believed that the leader must be respected. If you do things right, if you show that you're good at your job, employees will admire you and follow you." I said looking for agreement.

"That is just the beginning. Leadership is never reactive. You cannot expect them to follow you just because you are good or the best at the task. You must make them follow you. Leadership is a decision, a personal choice rather than a capability. You must be proactive and make them follow you. Remember that effectiveness is skill or technique, but it depends on motivation." He said.

-Right. The output of a team is equal to their capacity multiplied by their motivation." I summarized in my engineer style.

"The leader's role is fundamental. The leader must clarify what must be done, must teach to do things right, must unite people in a single direction, idea or a value and must be a motivator." Advised Mwalimu.

"What strikes me the most is that you always talk about leadership as a means to improve the team. Always working to develop it. Sometimes the skill improves, other times solidarity does. In my country many bosses prevent their teams from growing." I was speaking of my past experiences.

"That is a mistake. A leader has to be the best. The leader who fears the growth of those below subordinates to them due to his fear, and therefore, over time he drops below them. The cubic leader improves the team because a leader knows what his team is worth, and that the better his team is, the more value his leadership has." He asserted. In addition, a true leader is built on a solid foundation, his principles and values. Once I saw a kongoni about to give birth. At that time the female buffalo was helpless. It could hardly move with a calf that hung from her body. Some leopards seized the opportunity and prepared to attack. Jumbe came and threw them violently. He knew that this new life would eventually become bigger food. Large predators attack the weakest prey, old, sick or injured, not to undermine the species. This would ensure future supply. And those are the values that make a leader be respected by others. A leader has to demonstrate confidence in what he does with knowledge and skill, but above all with integrity."

"I couldn't agree more. The hard part is knowing with certainty what integrity is." I answered.

"Integrity is something very simple that we try to hide behind complexities. Integrity is simply doing what is expected of us. Doing what you preach and setting an example for others." He said with a smile.

"I could not agree more. There is nothing worse than a person who lacks confidence, especially if it is someone to follow. Employees, teams, need to feel confident, certain, and that the person who guides them needs to show them certainty, even if mistaken."

At that time the nurse entered the room with lunch. The morning had vanished in a flash, but I'll remember that conversation forever.

"It's time to go. Tomorrow we'll drive to the airport if you plan to still take the flight back." Mwalimu said in hurry, looking first at me and then at Mbuto so that he would hear his words.

"Perfect, don't worry, I am not taking off; I will wait here for you" I said, hiding my sadness at the irony. I really enjoyed listening to their stories, and at the same time I realized that during those days I had done something that had almost forgotten, stopping to think. Reconsidering behavior is an essential task for continuous improvement. The bad news is almost always, we are too busy to have time to think and what is worse is that most of the time that occupation is because we have not reflected at all.

XI.

The farewell

"Jambo." Mbuto and Mwalimu chanted in unison when they entered the room.

"Jambo." I replied, returning an African greeting we just used for the first time. I thought they just wanted to show me their closeness. The two wore a red robe, which I interpreted as if to give meaning to that ceremonious day. I had gotten used to that in Mwalimu, but Mbuto seemed another person wearing the traditional clothes.

I was still checking the suitcase with the intention of leaving everything I did not need. Not many things were useful in my city, so I decided to give them to Mbuto. I told him that share among his colleagues with the hidden intention for him to keep most of them without hurting his pride. I then left my professional safari greeting, which, along with my obvious ignorance, increased my image of an inexperienced neophyte.

The plane was leaving in three hours, so there was enough time, but we decided to go to the airport to avoid unnecessary stress, and why not, because I was sick of those hospital walls.

The road to the airport was not bad, but was limited to a ten-mile long strip of asphalt sprinkled with some billboards of Western products that few people had access to. It lacked lighting and protective measures, as there was not much traffic in that road at night and the cars were slow enough that it would nothing more than an expendable extra.

Mbuto drove the old SUV, which showed his social class once more. On the road a taxi was ahead of us, the rest were tourists' buses or dala-dala, a kind of public transport van where the local natives crowded.

The airport was not large or luxurious; as usual all kinds of people were there: happy couples and tourists from Zanzibar, adventurers who had climbed Kilimanjaro, Western businessmen, pro-Western and traditional natives clearly differentiated by their clothing, photo hunters, and of course, Dr. Livingston's fans.

It was too soon, but enough to still miss the crowd of casual travelers slowing the lines with questions and unimportant issues, so I it did not take me long to get my boarding pass and check the meager luggage that had survived my screening. I was left with just a small backpack, along with a camera and an mp3 with my favorite soundtracks, which accompanied me on all trips, especially to avoid listening to the conversations of other travelers; I deposited the eight wooden cubes, the eight pieces that I had hunted on my visit and the notebook with my notes.

Then we went to the checkpoint, where all passengers were searched to access the transit zone. I thought I would again repeat the routine of all my trips, buy a magazine that I really did not want to read, to keep abreast of current business, a bottle of mineral water, some sweet and certainly, a book that inspired me. At the end of the day, this was about an eight-hour trip that I spend as comfortable as possible.

There was still enough time before take off, so before crossing into the lane for passengers with boarding passes, we decided to sit a while in the cafeteria.

Until then, the three of us had spent an uneasy and sad silence, broken only by brief phrases essential only for proper invoicing procedures. Although it had been just over a week, I appreciated those two people. I had not dealt with people of integrity who enjoyed doing what they thought was right, not looking to get something in return, who gathered qualities and virtues and did not require that life would reward them, but who wanted to build their own.

"I think I will miss you when I get home." I told them honestly as they served coffee.

"Yes, I had been thinking that too. Talking to you offers me another perspective that helps me understand and develop mine." Mwalimu said, while Mbuto smiled and bowed his head sadly. He was also going to miss me.

"You have taught me a lot about how to lead my teams. Now it is very clear to me how to make them follow me." I said hastily.

"Careful, my friend. Leadership is not making them follow you, but getting them to want to follow you." He explained patiently.

"Excuse me, it is true. A good leader is not the one who requires doing things, but he who gets them to do them on their own motivation." I corrected.

"Yes it is true that the true leader knows when to demand, command, and does so with the intent to clarify, to correct or provide confidence for the team." He smiled.

"How important it is being a good leader!" I retracted in a whisper.

"Yes, and how important the team is. A leader is nothing without it. This is often forgotten by the false leaders." He scolded.

"How often they claim to be good managers or leaders, when in fact a leader is worth exactly what his team is worth. One without the other does not exist. How often do they complain about the team, and how few times do they ask what have they done to develop it? A person can have a brilliant mind and, most importantly, a strong heart, but if you have bad knees you cannot run. Then, we can heal the wound and keep running. The heart and mind are nothing without the leg, see?" He said, looking at my leg.

"Yes, it is clear. The leader and his associates must form one body. Have synergy and care about each other to achieve the best results." I said.

"But before you go, answer me one question: we have seen that teams are ranked according to three axes, what do you think is the most important?"

"Well, the leader's acceptance for one, solidarity between team members and the skill or confidence in their work. If we talk about leadership they must accept the leader.

"Yes, but a team is not a team if they are not united and do not cooperate among themselves." He interrupted.

"And it is the same whether they do it if they do not know what to do; so the most important axis is skill." I said.

"Indeed, the first thing to do is to have a base, which they know how to work. They will never accept the leader if they fail to score with him." He said.

"You cannot motivate in failure." I pointed out.

"Yes, it is difficult to run if you don't know the route or have a clear goal." He said.

"Sure, and once you have the knowledge, you win their acceptance." I said enthusiastically.

"Not so fast. Knowledge is not so important. Have you ever done things contrary to reason? Have you not done something crazy and you knew it was wrong or inappropriate?" He suggested.

"Yes, yes I replied, although I would like to tell you otherwise. Many times, however, the things I remember best are usually the ones that motivate me the most."

"It's normal. The human is gets swayed more by emotion than by reason. Try to explain things to a child," and he pointed to one that pulled the skirt of his mother;" and you will achieve little, but according to your tone of voice you will achieve on effect or another. Many times we do not hear what others say to us, but how they say it." He explained.

"Now, that is, the heart has its reasons of which reason knows nothing" I was quoting Blaise Pascal.

"Yes, and remember that the heart is the boss. The head helps us do things well, but for that, I must first want to do them." He said.

"I think, therefore I am. I feel, then I do." I thought.

"Then the next most important axis is?" He asked again.

"Umm, a team gets better performance when its members are united. Otherwise it's a mess that hinders each other. But on the other hand, if they do not accept the leader, they just end up doing what they want and can go in the opposite direction to that intended." I said before taking a sip of the great African coffee to be able to think before answering.

"Yes, and a leader can make the team go against him if he is too dominant." He said, while I savored the infusion.

"So the most important thing is to get the solidarity of the team. A leader must ensure that in a team, the whole forms something greater than the sum of the components. In the end, if there is no union, there is no team." I said, not without any doubt.

"Good. It is evident that the three axes are important, but acceptance of the leader must come from the other two, therefore, by being perhaps the most critical one, it is the third. Get your acceptance without attaining the skill to unite or without partners is not leading a team. In fact, it is to convey the individuality of a person to others." He said.

"Sure, and if this is missing, the rest are lost." I said, since I understood the reasoning.

"Of course. Also, if he achieves that the team learns and obtains skills, and if it becomes their role model, if he transfers a vision and common goals, and ensures that they can identify and pursue all together, the leader himself would get them to follow him and accept his orders and suggestions. Leadership, rather than an ambition is a consequence." He ended.

Absorbed, I held the cup of coffee in the air trying to remember the conversation to enter it later in my notebook. The three axes: skill, solidarity and acceptance. I will never forget them.

"Well, I think that although we do not want, it is time for you to prepare to leave." He said, returning me to reality. Mbuto looked at me with pity and smiled again.

"Yes, true." I said, and drank up the coffee before standing leaning my arm on my crutches.

I stopped just a few yards before the security gate where I had to render the crutch, and I first hugged Mbuto and then Mwalimu.

I hope to see them again someday. Anyway, here is my information, and if you ever need anything don't hesitate to contact me." I said, and gave them my card.

"Thanks, I will, and I hope you recover." Mwalimu said politely.

They waited until I got over the checkpoint. I walked away from the access corridor to the waiting area while answering back to their looks with mine in an attempt to retain their image. Deep down, I wondered if I would ever see them again.

XII.

The table

The return trip on the plane was too heavy. Usually, flights never overwhelm me, but during that flight, I could not get off the seat because I had to leave the crutches at the gate. Furthermore, no I did not have a single book with me, so I started to make drawings on cubes and more cubes arranged on three axes. Each time I drew a cube, I thought of the different parts of my organization. The nyoka, the chui, and so on, and gradually I completed the whole organization.

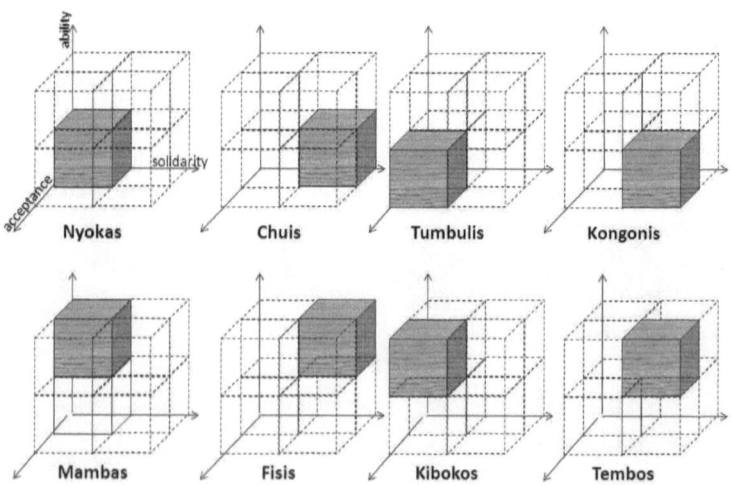

Now it was clear to me what I had to do with each of them. When I got tired of drawing, I set forth in a table my conclusions about cubic leadership. This table would be my plan of action to lead the company. I felt that dividing the company into groups and analyzing their characteristics, I could better understand each of them and better choose my behavior towards them.

Finally, it all fit together, each piece was in its place forming something greater than the sum of all the pieces.

NYOKAS	CHUIS	TUMBULIS	KONGONIS
Disoriented	**Insecures**	**Dependents**	**Gregarious**
They don't know how to do the work. Each goes its own way. They don't follow the leader	They work together but don't achieve the goals. They have difficulties to accept the orders of the leader	They can't do the work perfectly and don't get along with each other or don't cooperate although they do the bidding.	They are very cooperative with each other and accept the orders but do not dominate their functions
Lowly skilled	Lowly skilled	Lowly skilled	Lowly skilled
Low solidarity	High solidarity	Low solidarity	High solidarity
Low acceptation	Low acceptation	High acceptation	High acceptation
Controlling	**Protecting**	**Reference**	**Guiding**
The leader establishes an efficient procedure.	The leader demands respect and controls from a distance.	The leader becomes the role model for the team.	The leader shows how to do tasks well, how to improve them.
He instructs mandatory rules.	Eventually, he defends the team.	He gives an example so that everyone knows what to do.	He innovates; discovers new things to others.
He provides a continuous presence.	He is a role model, his behavior is an example, and he teaches and transmits.	He becomes the lead player.	Enthusiastically, he presents a vision, a future.
He establishes a rapid response control.	He ensures that the team is trained.	He gets the results one by one.	He celebrates and enjoys success, publicly and notoriously.
He treats everyone equally.	He shares success.	He makes sure the team achieves the results and monitors.	He creates team synergy and avoids any differences.

MAMBAS	FISIS	KIBOKOS	TEMBOS
Specialists	Insatiable	Stucker	PreLeader
They do the things but do not collaborate among themselves and accept the orders of the leader	They are very good at his job and in fact they could brag about it. Because of it they are very closed. In other way they use to discuss the orders of the leader	They do a good work but they look bored. Distrust between them and often complain much. Still following the leader and his orders	They have great skill and confidence in themselves, relate well with others and agree to leader but are afraid of losing their status.
Highly skilled	Highly skilled	Highly skilled	Highly skilled
Low solidarity	High solidarity	Low solidarity	High solidarity
Low acceptation	Low acceptation	High acceptation	High acceptation
Participating	Mastering	Cohesive	Sponsoring
The leader has a vision that goes beyond his scope of work.	The leader shows the example instead of demanding action, he becomes the example and shows how to achieve results.	The leader prevents and controls conflict, suspicion and envy.	The leader must be able to train and promote new leaders.
He communicates that vision to the team to be aware of its importance.	He reconciles his own gains with the gains of the team.	He creates group identity, establishing a goal or a common mission.	He has to offer them safety from a distance.
What motivates the team is not a person but the mission and the objective pursued.	The leader is the one who makes them win. With him they get results.	He imposes a group task, for the members to interact and help.	He sets the expected results, but lets the new leader establish its own mechanisms.
The leader must be able to identify the strengths and weaknesses of the team members.	He shares success, he is one of them when it comes to working, and also when is time to enjoy success.	He changes the routine to make work fun.	He controls and assists when necessary.
He participates in the team's activities and gets involved, but he allows everyone to do their job.	He commits not only to working or to the goal, but also with the team members.	He makes a joint celebration, even outside the common area	He lets them make mistakes, and corrects them.

Glossary

Chui: leopard

Duma: cheetah

Erevu: knowledge

Fisi: Hyena

Jumbe: leader

Kabila: tribe, solidarity

Kiboko: hippopotamus

Kongoni: gnu, wildebeest

Kun: chief

Mamba: crocodile

Mfalme: king

Mlima: mountain

Msaada: assistant

Mte: tree

Mwalimu: Professor, teacher

Ndovu: elephant

Nyoka: snake

Nyumba: house

Nyumbu: gnu, wildebeest

Paa: gazelle

Pokea: accept

Punda milia: zebra

Rafiki: friend, friendship

Simba: lion

Tembo: elephant

Tumbuli: monkey

The author

Daniel Andrino has a master's degree in HR Management from San Pablo CEU Business School and is Bachelor of Arts in Industrial Sociology. Furthermore he studied at Stanford Center for Professional Development and INSEAD. He was responsible for selection and internal communication at KPMG Consulting, senior consultant of Management Development at Unisys Consulting and Telvent, training coordinator at Securitas Direct, Project Manager at Crossknowledge and currently works at Human Resource Department of Isolux. He has lectured at the Complutense University of Madrid, San Pablo CEU Business School, ITAE, Polytechnic University of Valencia, and the Graduate Institute of the Comillas Pontifical University ICAI-ICADE.

Contact him at <u>daniel.andrino@liderazgocubico.com</u>